THE NEW BOSS HAS A MILK MUSTACHE

My Promotion to Motherhood

Leola Floren

Beacon Hill Press of Kansas City
Kansas City, Missouri

Copyright 1996
by Beacon Hill Press of Kansas City

ISBN 083-411-576X

Printed in the
United States of America

Cover Design: Ted Ferguson
Cover Photo: Comstock

All Scripture quotations not otherwise designated are from the *Holy Bible, New International Version*® (NIV®). Copyright © 1973, 1978, 1984 by International Bible Society. Used by permission of Zondervan Publishing House. All rights reserved.

Permission to quote from the following additional copyrighted version of the Bible is acknowledged with appreciation:

The Living Bible (TLB), © 1971. Used by permission of Tyndale House Publishers, Inc., Wheaton, IL 60189. All rights reserved.

Scripture quotation marked KJV is from the King James Version.

Library of Congress Cataloging-in-Publications Data
Floren, Leola, 1953-
    The new boss has a milk mustache : my promotion to motherhood / Leola Floren.
       p.   cm.
    ISBN 0-8341-1576-X (pbk.)
    1. Motherhood—United States. 2. Motherhood—Religious aspects—Christianity.   I. Title.
HQ759.F58 1996
248.8'431—dc20   96-7097
                                                       CIP

To my husband,
Wyatt,
whose hard work and commitment
to family
make it possible
for me to be
a full-time mom

November 1996

To Karen,

Super mom, superfriend! Thank you for all you do and all you are... in the name of our Heavenly parent.

Love,
Linda

Contents

Preface	7
1. Good-bye, Corporate World; Hello, Graham Crackers	9
2. Mom: Promotion or Demotion?	18
3. The Rabbit Ate My Day Planner	27
4. Getting Along with a Difficult Coworker (The One I Married)	38
5. You Can Blame the Bottom Line on Toilet Fairies	49
6. All Stressed Out and No Place to Go	56
7. My Power Suit Is Low on Batteries	66
8. The Custodial Staff Is on Strike, and Company's Coming	76
9. Please Hold My Calls—Someone Just Smeared Vaseline Over the Electrical Outlet	84
10. My Prayers Are Hitting the Glass Ceiling	92
11. The CEO Has a Sense of Humor	102
12. Is There Life After Rush Hour?	112
Notes	119

PREFACE

The going rate for teen baby-sitters in my subdivision is $4 an hour. I found this out at the worst possible moment—while driving the sitter home. At that wage, as the full-time mother of a 10-year-old, I should be roughly $350,000 ahead by now. But of course nobody pays moms $4 an hour to take care of their own kids.

In an era in which an individual's worth too often is measured by the income she generates, it takes a great deal of commitment for a woman to take time off from a career in order to rear a family. It is those women for whom this book was written, and it is those women I wish to thank.

In my immediate family I count my mother, Nadine Floren, and sister, Arline Floren Proctor, as two such women, as well as my mother-in-law, Bonnie Gee. Several fine teachers have modeled biblically based motherhood to me, and specifically I would like to acknowledge Betty King, Dorcas Hamlet, and Glaphré Gilliland. Though she is not a biological mother, Glaphré has served as a spiritual mother to thousands through teaching and Prayerlife Ministries.

Finally, I would like to thank the scores of women who have shared coffee and advice with me over the years. When you're exhausted and the diaper pail is ready to explode with toxic Pampers, it's good to know that others have been there, and not only survived, but thrived.

Here's to you, Mom.

1

Good-bye, Corporate World; Hello, Graham Crackers

It was 10:51 a.m. on a Monday, and I sat at my desk gasping for breath, trying not to look winded. I'd left the house at 8:09, but, thanks to a detour made necessary because the regular baby-sitter had the flu, it took me slightly more than two and a half hours to get to work. Graham cracker crumbs as thick as volcanic ash coated the interior of my car; spilled milk stained my skirt; a hole in my stocking, the size of a quarter, grew larger by the minute; and my sandwich had been smashed when I set my briefcase on top of it. Welcome to the exciting, fast-paced, glamorous world of the working mother.

That myth is one of the main reasons women grit their teeth and roll their eyes when TV models with perfect hair and no runs in their pantyhose pretend to drop off perfectly happy children at perfect child care centers. Those of us who have ridden the daycare roller coaster, or have scrambled to find a replacement when the baby-sitter was sick, know better.

When I experienced that disastrous Monday several years ago, I had already trimmed my work schedule to one office day a week. As a columnist for a metropolitan daily newspaper, I had the flexibility to do most of my work at home and planned to continue that schedule until my daughter was in school. Management had other ideas, however. The new editor who took over my department saw no connection between issues that affected my growing family—the issues I wanted to write about—and issues that affect society at large.

I would have to accept a new assignment, she insisted, and my days of working at home were over. Faced with the prospect of placing my two-year-old daughter in full-time day care, I made the easiest decision of my career: I quit.

The financial consequence was drastic and immediate. While my husband and I had determined at the outset of our marriage that we would never grow dependent upon two incomes, it was still a shock when that first payless Thursday rolled around, followed by another and another. There were other adjustments as well.

Knowing you've made the right choice for yourself and your family doesn't automatically make the transition easy. What happened over a period of many months and years is that God began to teach me—and He teaches me still—that things of lasting importance are often ignored or discounted by society. Politicians pay great lip service to traditional values, but their policies and programs make it difficult for women to stay home and raise their children.

A major corporation establishes a daycare center on the premises, and many cheer, as if somehow a working parent can pack a day's worth of "quality time" into a couple of coffee breaks and a lunch hour. Those of us who have been there understand that quality time requires *quantity* time, because toddlers don't schedule their moments of need and awareness according to Mom's day planner.

Consequently, I traded a boss in a conservative three-piece suit for a boss with a milk mustache. I've never regretted the decision, but I'll admit there are things I miss about the corporate world—long lunches in nice restaurants with coworkers, enough money in the checking account to pay full price for a perfect pair of pumps, frequent compliments on my work.

Those pleasures are rare for stay-at-home moms, and, at the risk of sounding a bit self-focused, some of them are hard to give up. When you've poured years of your life into preparing for a career and then find that you need to take a leave of absence for a decade or more, it's tough.

This book is for women who prepared for careers in the marketplace and now find themselves devoted to home and family. The transition isn't always easy, but whatever the stage—whether you have a little one on the way, or a little one napping right now so you can read for 57 blessed uninterrupted minutes, or children who are older and in school—God's Word has much to teach us about how to use what we've learned in the workplace: "Only be careful, and watch yourselves closely so that you do not forget the things your eyes have seen or let them slip from your heart as long as you live. Teach them to your children and to their children after them" (Deut. 4:9).

Our Children: Whose Values Will They Absorb?

I haven't had a nap since 1987, shortly after my daughter, Lauren, learned to string words together into complete sentences and, looking at me with tenderness, said, "I wish you'd go to sleep, Mommy, so I could cut your hair."

Could this be the child for whom I, like Hannah, had so fervently prayed?

I thought back to a day long before when she was only a few weeks old, still puny-voiced and with feet the size of a Cabbage Patch Kid's, and the United States Postal Service delivered a book sent by my friend Glaphré. It was a gift book, the kind you can purchase in stationery stores, and all its pages were blank.

On the inside cover Glaphré had written a note to my little girl, but I had a feeling I was supposed to read it too. "Dear Lauren," it said. "This is for you! It's for your mom to write in—to write some of the special things that happen to you and for you. To write some of the special times you minister to other people, even as a baby. So that later—when you're older—you can read through this book and know that even from the beginning God had His special hand of blessing on YOU."

So that was it. A spiritual diary for a child. A great idea, I thought; and I promptly stuck it in the "get to eventually" stack of papers in an out-of-the-way drawer. There it sat for three years. Occasionally, while rummaging for a misplaced birth certificate or immunization chart, I would notice it, the butterflies on its colorful cover filling me with shame.

What was I to write? Lauren went to Sunday School when she was 11 days old, and smiled at strangers in elevators, and brightened up the nursing home when we visited an elderly friend. But where were the great moments of spiritual discovery and growth worthy of being recorded in a book? Told that God is a spirit and is with us wherever we go, even in the car, her question was, as ever, most practical: "Is He wearing His seat belt?" I was beginning to wonder when there would be anything to write in the diary.

Like most parents who want their children to love and trust God from the earliest possible moment, my husband, Wyatt, and I prayed with our daughter nearly every night before she went to bed. We prayed for her friends and sick people we knew and family members and the nightmares that sometimes frightened her and whatever else she wanted us to pray about. But when it was her turn, she would thank God that Mommy was going to take her for ice cream the following day—a type of spiritual blackmail that didn't seem worthy of recording in the diary.

Then one afternoon in the spring, the Thursday before Easter, we wrapped ourselves in layers of sweaters and socks, pulled on our coats, and headed for the skating rink in a nearby town. My husband plays ice hockey on a company team, and Lauren and I decided to go along and cheer. Actually, I went to cheer—she went for the popcorn from the snack bar and the vending machine bubble gum.

Not very many wives and kids show up for the games, so there were perhaps a dozen fans in the bleachers, including a woman with two small boys. Lauren, who has no trouble breaking into a locked room or a conversation, marched up the bleachers, wedged herself between the mother and one of her sons, and offered to share her candy and popcorn.

Before long the woman began asking Lauren questions about the upcoming holiday. "Do you know how many days until the Easter bunny comes?" she said, smiling. "Are you going to get an Easter basket from the bunny?"

And then my daughter, whose eyes glazed over like a blank TV screen every time we tried to talk about deep spiritual matters, looked at this stranger with kindness and wonder and said simply, "Jesus died for you and me."

None of the rest of us could think of a thing to say, for a child with popcorn on her chin had spoken the most important truth ever heard within that skating rink. She *had* listened. She *had* learned. She *had* absorbed the dozens of Bible stories and conversations as we walked from the car to the park slide and back again. She understood the meaning of Easter, and the good news had spilled out of her mouth as naturally and gracefully as water splashing from a fountain.

What a joy it was to hear the greatest message the world has ever known falling from the lips of my child!

Compared to that moment, the missing Thursday paychecks are insignificant. If I had chosen my career, I would have missed the miracle of His handiwork.

Piecing the Quilt of Childhood

Though I'm not one myself, I come from a long line of quilters. My mother and grandmothers and great-grandmothers all pieced together leftover fabric scraps, fashioning asymmetrical mosaics from worn dresses, aprons, shirts, and linens. Family members still curl up in those quilts to ward off chill in the wintertime, and when I unfold each one in the fall, I love scanning it for familiar slivers of history.

The brown calico is from my favorite dress in junior high school; and the white cotton with tiny pears, apples, and lemons is from a jumper my mother made when I was in elementary school. Another floral print is all that remains of matching dresses my mother, sister, and I wore to church in the early 1960s.

Perhaps the most important lesson of a quilt is that no scrap, however small, is ever wasted or unimportant. That is the lesson of motherhood. Every hour spent reading fairy tales or Bible stories to a toddler is worthwhile and of lasting value. Every lunch of peanut butter on toast or peanut butter on celery or peanut butter on the kitchen floor is one more piece in the fabric that will eventually form the quilt of a person's childhood.

Who will stitch together the pieces of your child's quilt? Teachers will enter his or her life with needle and thread, as will grandparents, aunts, uncles, brothers, sisters, neighbors, friends, baby-sitters, choir directors, coaches, and scores of others. But the keepers of the quilt—Mom and Dad—are entrusted with a task of far more lasting impact than the actual stitching.

We arrange the pieces, looking for attractive patterns

here and there, screening scraps in order to discard pieces that are too frayed, cutting other pieces to fit. As we mold and direct our children's activities, and nurture and encourage their God-given interests and talents, we slowly help them design the pattern of their quilts. In the early years, we place each piece where we want it; later, the child begins to offer opinions. ("More blue, please. I don't like that yellow piece—it's scratchy!") Sometimes, even though it makes us cringe, we let our children choose a color or pattern that we know is less than perfect, because we want them to learn that every scrap carries a lifelong consequence.

The more time we spend with them, the more opportunities we have to guide them as they select their pieces. That is one of the main reasons I'm a stay-at-home mom. Twenty years from now when I look at my child's quilt, I want to remember where each piece came from and know I had a hand in it.

Using Your Work Skills in the Home

I spent 6 years in college and 11 years on the job learning to be a journalist. When it came to the most important job of my life—that of mother—I went into it completely untrained.

At least that's how it felt at first. I didn't know anything about feedings, diapers, sleeping patterns, or rectal thermometers. Amazingly, the baby survived, and so did I (though a number of the thermometers were unfortunate casualties). Over time I realized that the skills I'd developed in my career served me well in the home. To be a good journalist you need to be a voracious reader, so I devoured books and articles on parenting. I practiced listening to my child as carefully as I had listened to story sources, asking questions as if she were the most important interview of my life, and as I did, I found her eager to share the deepest thoughts in her heart.

Finally, I began to write. Just as Glaphré suggested, I wrote of the impact Lauren had on people's lives, even as a baby and a toddler. When my daughter looks back on the first 16 years of her life, I can't imagine she'll want to read the hundreds of newspaper and magazine articles I wrote about other people, places, and things. She'll be fascinated, though, by the bits and pieces of memory that tell the story of her own life and of her physical and spiritual development.

You, too, have special talents and abilities with which you can have an impact on your child's life. The skills you developed in school and in the workplace can be invaluable in the home. Are you a super organizer? Consider organizing a baby-sitting co-op in the neighborhood. Are you a gifted teacher? Use that talent to teach your own child. Are you a musician? Fill your home with a joyful noise, and guide those small, precious hands to the piano keys or to the strings of a violin. Do you love to sing? Sing in the car, in the aisles of the supermarket, in line at the post office.

Whatever you have learned to do, use those skills to enrich the lives of your children. When you do this, you're investing in a project of eternal value. What's a paycheck, compared with that?

Bottom Line

List the top five skills you possess(ed) as an employee, manager, or business owner:

1.

2.

3.

4.

5.

Ask God to reveal to you ways in which those skills can be used to enrich the lives of your children and make you a better parent.

2

Mom: Promotion or Demotion?

I WAS CERTAIN I'D NEVER GET ANOTHER FULL NIGHT'S SLEEP.

For 11 months after the baby was born, I was up at least once a night, often long enough to catch the entire 3 A.M. *Eight Is Enough* rerun, an old series about a family with eight children. At that hour *one* is enough—more than enough.

Just when I began to think I'd need a can of spackling compound to cover the circles under my eyes, inconsiderate relatives taught the baby to walk. From that point on, no nook or cranny in the house was safe from exploring fingers.

On the eve of her second birthday, Lauren tried to flush a stuffed penguin down the toilet. It was also at about this age that she discovered that the dining room chandelier would swing if she climbed onto the table and gave it a shove.

I forgot what it was like to run to the supermarket for a gallon of milk. Every shopping expedition took at least two hours and required 15 pounds of luggage, including a stroller from which Houdini could not have escaped. Lauren wiggled out as soon as I turned my back.

Long before her third birthday she gave up naps and followed me everywhere, and I sent a donation to public television; because if it hadn't been for *Mister Rogers' Neighborhood,* I never could have showered alone.

The summer she turned four, I wasn't able to unload the dishwasher without being summoned outside by a plaintive "Mommmmmy!" She wanted to swing but couldn't pump. She wanted to catch frogs, but they were too fast. She wanted to explore the universe but wasn't allowed past the next-door neighbor's driveway.

Then, that fall, she entered preschool. Three afternoons a week, for a total of seven and a half hours, she was someone else's responsibility, and I felt I had all the time in the world. To celebrate, I went to Wendy's, ordered a taco salad, and read a book without pictures. I devoured my freedom as if it were chocolate cake, savoring each bite and looking forward to the next slice.

Before I knew it, Lauren turned five. I didn't think about it being a milestone until she opened a birthday card and five one-dollar bills fell out. The realization hit hard: In a few weeks she would climb onto a school bus with a name tag pinned to her shirt and return a few hours later, transformed. Already I could hear her telling me, "But my teacher says . . ." in the same stubborn tone that I had educated my own mother.

That summer she crossed the street after looking both ways. She didn't need me to push her on the swing anymore, and she even managed to catch a frog. Before too many more summers passed, I would be out of a job.

A job—what an odd way to think of mothering. After five years of 24-hour shifts, I not only didn't have a pension, but I was also at the same hourly rate—zilch—that I had been when I took the assignment. I had no paid vacations or sick days, and the benefits were hit-and-miss: a hug here, a kiss there, an invitation to share a bag of M & M's—as long as I was buying.

Out of curiosity I did some figuring. Giving up a full-time career to spend the first five years of this child's life with her had cost in the neighborhood of $175,000. If I had that much in the bank, I'd never clip another coupon or buy discount underwear. If mothering is a job, not only am I not on the fast track but I've been run over by a semi.

Let's not kid ourselves. It can be stressful staying home with little ones, when the exciting and financially rewarding things in life seem to be happening in the "work" world. As mothers, we can't look forward to promotions, and most of us won't be taking leisurely child-free vacations for a couple of decades. If we once worked in careers in which we reaped positive feedback, whether in the form of memos, phone calls from grateful clients, or fan mail, full-time mothering might actually feel like a demotion.

Business-oriented individuals, though, know the value of weighing pros and cons and gathering all the data before drawing conclusions. With that in mind, let's look at a "typical" workday in the life of a stay-at-home mom.

Life Without Coffee Breaks

At 6:30 A.M., Mrs. Dobbs stumbles out of bed, having already been up twice during the night, and discovers that because of a leaky diaper (to say nothing of a leaky baby), the crib sheets are soaked. After feeding the baby, feeding Mr. Dobbs, hustling the sheets into the laundry room, and gargling a quick shot of Scope in order to clear the fuzz out of her mouth, she grabs a two-minute shower before Mr. Dobbs leaves for work, and emerges to find a soggy spot on the den carpet where the baby threw up.

After getting dressed and cleaning up the mess and the baby, she spends the rest of the morning sorting coupons, paying bills, doing dishes and laundry, straightening the bathroom, making the bed, and tracking down a wayward catalog order on the telephone. Just when the buzzer goes off on the dryer the baby starts to cry, so she fixes a bowl of rice cereal, puts on her full-length rubber apron, and manages to get half the cereal into the baby before he sneezes, splattering the four corners of the kitchen and Mrs. Dobbs from the neck up.

By the time she gets back to the laundry, Mr. Dobbs's wool-and-polyester slacks have taken on the look of a topographical map of the Himalayas, so she irons them. After a quick lunch of Pop-Tarts, eaten while standing at the sink, she tiptoes into the nursery to check on the napping baby, only to bash her toe on the crib. Since the baby is awake anyway, she bundles him up for a fast trip to the supermarket that takes three hours—because it *takes* three hours when you're shopping with a baby.

After putting away the groceries, she sets the baby into his swing, sinks onto the couch, exhausted, picks up yesterday's newspaper, and props her feet on the table—at exactly the moment Mr. Dobbs walks in.

"Glad to see you were able to relax today," says Mr. Dobbs.

While he plays with the baby, she washes the cereal from her hair before the sitter (whom it has taken Mrs. Dobbs seven calls to find) arrives. Finally, it's off to a party hosted by Mr. Dobbs's boss.

Now visualize the weary Mrs. Dobbs, cornered by one of her husband's chatty coworkers who casually remarks, "I understand you're enjoying the life of a homemaker. It's nice you were able to quit working." Even though no jury of her peers would convict her, Mrs. Dobbs wisely resists the impulse to choke him.

Mothering is hard, demanding, usually thankless work. Shaping the values and self-esteem of a child is an exciting occupation, but let's face the facts: On many days, most of our time is eaten up by unglamorous chores, cleanup duty, and meal preparation that nobody is going to remember and hardly anyone thinks to appreciate.

A homemaker friend of mine recalls a conversation years ago at a dinner party, in which a career woman actually had the nerve to say, "Boy, you've really had a free ride all these years."

"Free ride, my foot!" the homemaker muttered many days later, recounting the incident with sparking eyes. This is a woman who bakes bread, makes her husband's neckties, sews her kids' pajamas, and knits their mittens. She's fed up with people who assume she lounges around all day, gorging on soap operas and Doritos.

She has, for 15 years, devoted her talents full time to family. Yet in some circles, because the check she carries to the bank bears her husband's name and endorsement, she's considered a freeloader. A few years ago, she was considered the ideal.

Is it any wonder she feels defensive when she hears that she isn't living up to her potential, that she's wasting these years and cheating herself and society out of a worthwhile contribution? She has two children whom she considers more-than-worthwhile contributions, plus a house and a husband, and they consume most of her time and energy.

"I think I work just as hard as people who are out getting paid for it," she says. "I paint and clean, keep the household accounts in order, help with homework, proofread and type papers, pay all the bills, do the banking, mow the lawn, rake the yard, decorate cakes for birthdays—see all these fun things homemakers can find to do?"

In addition, she operates the family shuttle between music lessons, libraries, and doctors' appointments; cooks; shops; and does volunteer work for school and church.

When the kids were babies she scorned disposable diapers as wasteful, washing cloth ones and hanging them to dry.

How much training and skill and stamina does it take to be a homemaker? Maybe I'll ask her on her next coffee break. So far, in 15 years, she hasn't taken one.

Mothering Is a Demanding Profession

The biggest boost to homemaking in the early 1990s came from a completely unexpected source: the women of Wellesley College. A widely publicized controversy developed when approximately 150 students protested the selection of first lady Barbara Bush as commencement speaker. Their objection? Mrs. Bush had dropped out of college, gotten married, and had a family instead of a career. Her power, they argued, was "derivative," and thus she had no business addressing a scholarly group of career-bound young women.

The Wellesley grads let it be known in no uncertain terms that they would rather hear from a woman of accomplishment, a worthy role model for the leaders of tomorrow. The problem was, they hadn't lived long enough to recognize valid credentials when they saw them.

At the time of the commencement flap, I took a look at Mrs. Bush's credentials, and I found her more than competent in several critical areas:

- **Psychology.** During her husband's presidential campaign she admitted that she looked older than he, wore fake pearls, and refused to dye her hair. For these reasons alone, I'm convinced that half the women who voted for George Bush in 1988 were actually voting for Barbara.

The 1990 graduates may have thought they would be judged strictly on academic excellence during their careers, but the sad fact is that most of the working world is obsessed with appearance. When Mrs. Bush refused to play the glamour game—turning the White House beauty parlor into a dog hospital, for instance—she in effect said, "I like the way I am. I earned every one of my wrinkles and every strand of my snowy hair, and if a toddler is going to take a fistful of pearls and snap the strand that binds them together, it'll be easier on everyone involved if they're from J. C. Penney instead of Tiffany's."

We could use more practical thinking like that in the business world.

- **Geography.** For several decades Mrs. Bush made a career of packing up and moving, as her husband bounced around the world honing his skills in business, foreign service, and politics. She must have spent a fortune having new address labels printed, a problem to which every transferred spouse in America can relate. Even more difficult, she found herself saying good-bye to comfortable homes and friendships, only to begin again somewhere else.

Flexibility and an ability to adapt to change are key ingredients in a successful career, whether you're running a home or corporation.

- **Literature.** Anyone who encourages parents to cuddle toddlers in their laps and read storybooks, as Mrs. Bush did, has a chance to accomplish some good in the world. It may not pack the wallop of a corporate takeover, but considering her salary, Mrs. Bush's war on illiteracy may have been the all-time best bargain in Washington.

- **Courage.** Years ago Mrs. Bush watched one of her children die. She experienced a grief too deep for words or comfort and emerged with her dignity and priorities intact. Like many who have suffered greatly, Mrs. Bush developed an understanding of what has value and what is simply window dressing. Women of that depth don't get distraught over bad hair days or malfunctioning fax machines.

Though she lacked a college degree, as first lady Mrs. Bush was wise in the ways of life. While many of us may have found ourselves disagreeing with her stand on specific social or political issues, her views on the importance of homemaking were as refreshing as a cool shower after a hike in the desert. She knew, as many of us do, that rearing children is an education in itself, and that to wear one's wrinkles proudly is no small accomplishment.

Years from now, will I wear my gray hair and mothering wrinkles proudly? The civic organizations that hand out plaques to successful business people aren't likely to give me an award; all the trophies I'm ever likely to get are already stashed in the bottom of the closet (and two of them are for bowling).

Is mothering a promotion or a demotion? The answer to that question varies, depending upon who you ask—150 women from the class of 1990 may consider it a demotion, but I defer to an authority who's been around the block a few times. When my retirement from active motherhood comes around in a few years, I hope to be able to speak these words from 3 John 4—"I have no greater joy than to hear that my children are walking in the truth."

As a parent, that's my career objective. Every story I read aloud, every snack I prepare, every sheet I change, every stuffed animal I rescue from the toilet bowl—in short, every task I attempt—should be approached with that goal in mind.

There are repetitive and boring chores to be done while my child is growing up, and in many cases I don't see the connection between those mindless tasks and eternal goals. Yet the small jobs are just as important as the large ones. The president of General Motors can't accomplish much of anything if the computer system is down or the switchboard operator misdirects incoming calls. When God is the CEO (Chief Executive Officer) of our homes and families, no assigned task, however seemingly insignificant, is ever wasted or unworthy of our attention and effort. Motherhood is the most important profession we will ever pursue, and when God blesses us with that assignment, we can rest assured we've gotten the best of all promotions.

A mother's work never has to be meaningless. As you make a child's bed, you can pray that the child will sleep peacefully—and always remember how important it is to end the day with a conversation with God. When you pack a school lunch or put money in a pocket or envelope, ask God to nourish the child's spirit as well as the body while he or she is at school. While you scrub the bathroom, ask God to show you any unclean areas in your own thought life, and ask Him for His cleansing.

Bottom Line

Make a list of the routine chores you'll do today. Ask God to show you the "bigger picture," or how you can minister to your loved ones through each of those jobs.

Job   *The Big Picture*

1. _____   _____

2. _____   _____

3. _____   _____

4. _____   _____

5. _____   _____

3

The Rabbit Ate My Day Planner

My friend Peter is thoroughly organized, plans his work and recreation schedules days in advance, and cannot stand to be one minute late for an appointment. Obviously, traffic jams, untimely phone calls, and other unpredictable events drive him crazy.

At least that's the way he *used* to be. Peter's firstborn, Nathan, helped change that.

When Nathan was a baby first learning to walk, Peter followed him all over the house with pillows. When Nathan staggered too close to stairs or the sharp edge of a table, Peter would drop a pillow into his path to redirect him gently, and also to cushion the blow if he should happen to fall.

Nathan was oblivious to his father's careful protection. Like other babies, he scrambled here, there, and everywhere, in search of adventures (which always seemed to involve sharp corners, stairs, or electrical outlets). Sometimes he cried when those annoying pillows got in his way. Sometimes he tried crawling over or around them. Sometimes he tumbled into them, laughing. He never figured out what they were for or who put them there.

Along the way, the pillow game began changing Peter's outlook on traffic jams and a lot of other things. What if, he reasoned, a loving Heavenly Father was dropping pillows into his path to redirect or protect *him?* What if the long line at the bank was that Father's way of keeping him out of an accident on the way home? What if that annoying dinnertime sales call was divinely timed to make sure he was still home for a much more important conversation?

What if the toddler who clung to his leg begging for just one more kiss and hug was God's pillow, a gentle redirection of thoughts, attitudes, and priorities?

Ever since Peter told me about his pillow revelation, I've been on the lookout for pillows in my own life. Sometimes they look like interruptions, and I'm tempted to complain and grow impatient; but when I do, I close my eyes and imagine our Heavenly Father. He's carefully watching each of my steps, mindful of my inexperience and blissful recklessness. He expects me to stumble now and then—as children do—but He's always there, guiding and directing with love and compassion.

God's Word says, "As a father has compassion on his children, so the LORD has compassion on those who fear him" (Ps. 103:13). As His children, we can count on Him to be with us and watch over us wherever we go. Unlike a human father, He will not allow us to wander from His presence, and His amazing pillows rescue us more times each day than we'll ever know. We can pray with confidence and assurance:

> *Heavenly Father,*
> *Thank You for pillows.*
> *I know You've dropped many of them*
> *into my path,*
> *and I mistook them*
> *for inconveniences.*
> *When I begin to feel frustrated*

> *with traffic jams
> that interfere with my schedule,
> remind me that You see clearly
> all that lies ahead,
> and I'd be wise to follow
> Your detours.*

When we lose sight of who God is, anxiety can grab hold and seize control of our thoughts and emotions. Being a world-class worrier myself, I know how easy it is to fall into the "What if?" trap—every possible disastrous scenario tap-dances through my imagination, until I'm paralyzed with fear.

Into this noisy and frightening mental torture chamber comes the quiet voice of One who says, "I am the LORD, the God of all mankind. Is anything too hard for me?" (Jer. 32:27). If I believe that, it has to make a difference in every significant area of my life.

A Rabbit Multiplies Trouble

That said, I have a confession to make. I hate interruptions, whether they take the form of a doorbell when I'm on a deadline, or a toddler with Cheeto-stained fingers crawling up my pant leg. The worst, though, was when my daughter's pet rabbit managed to disable $4,000 worth of computer equipment.

Now, many rabbits make fine house pets, and I've been in homes in which the family rabbit hopped from one room to another hoping to find a compassionate human who might scratch it behind the ears or fetch it a carrot. Unfortunately, the gray-eared California rabbit that my daughter named Snowmobile could not have cared less whether anyone scratched him behind the ears. He was too busy chewing on electrical cords to notice.

In many respects, he was much like a human toddler. He wandered this way and that looking for something interesting, and when he found it, he clamped onto it with his teeth. That's why I always kept an eye on him on those rare occasions when he was out of his cage.

Did I say "always"? One morning, deep in thought, I was vaguely aware that Snowmobile was no longer napping on the floor beside my foot and was instead investigating the tangle of wires under the desk that connected keyboard, computer terminal, printer, modem, telephone, and answering machine, each one a lifeline to the newspapers for which I do freelance work.

Startled, I shooed him into the open and frantically began examining the wires, while behind my back he quietly did unspeakable things to the stack of paperwork, phone messages, and the prioritized "to do" schedule I'd dropped beside my chair.

When my husband came home that night, I greeted him with as much cheer as I could dredge up from the pit of despair: "First the good news: Nobody was electrocuted." (After 13 years of marriage, I know how to get the guy's attention.)

Thanks to the resident engineer and his trusty toolbox, the repairs weren't extensive or terribly expensive, and the computer was up and running again in a matter of hours. All my worry and anxiety had been a waste of time, because things worked out for the best after all. My next newspaper article was on "The Perils of Rabbits as House Pets."

How many times have I worked myself into a full-fledged state of anxiety because things didn't go according to plan? Hundreds. And how many times has God, the Master Engineer, reached into my life with tender, skilled hands, repaired the broken components, and restored my system to full power? Too many to count.

In the midst of a carefully planned day filled with interruptions (and there aren't many days without at least a dozen), it's wise to remember that no surprises come into our lives except those that God allows. It's particularly important to remember that fact when your schedule is turned upside down by "little" interruptions, like the girl I'll call Lindsey.

When Opportunity Knocks at the Wrong Time

Lindsey was at the door. Again. It was the third afternoon in a row she had arrived as my preschooler and I were finishing our lunch. I didn't know her last name and had only a vague notion of where she lived.

The day before, I had asked if she knew her phone number, and when she gave it to me I called her mother. I introduced myself and asked if Lindsey could play inside.

"Sure," came the reply. "She's down there all the time anyway."

I took that to mean that the mother had set fairly general guidelines concerning staying within the city limits and then had sent her on her way. Lindsey was five years old.

In the previous two days I'd learned that Lindsey liked to play with stickers, Silly Putty, my daughter's dolls, and a game called "Pizza Party." She also liked apples and didn't care much about sharing.

That's about all I knew about this young houseguest, even though on her second afternoon in my home she had stayed five hours. Right before supper, I had suggested that she call her mother to see if it might be time to go home. In the meantime I had supervised games, provided snacks, and refereed arguments.

Day three of "Operation: Lindsey" was more of the same, and I caught myself thinking, "This isn't fair! I quit my job in order to take care of my daughter, not the whole neighborhood!" I guess I was still reeling from a little boy I'll call Frank, who had been a regular visitor for a couple of years until his family moved.

There were many weeks during which I know I spent more time with Frank than his parents did, and sometimes I resented it. He didn't know how to put on his jacket, so I taught him. He didn't know how to tie his shoes, so I tied them—again and again and again, holding my breath because his socks gave off fumes that would have stunned a camel. I fed him more crackers and cookies and glasses of milk than you can imagine, and then one day he invited himself to stay for lunch.

The peanut-butter-and-jelly sandwiches were on the table and Frank had started to dig in when I said, "Frank, we say thanks before we eat."

Frank turned his dark, bewildered, four-year-old eyes up at me and said soberly, "Thanks."

It was an honest and innocent misunderstanding, but it stunned me. Frank had no idea what it meant to pray before meals, or any other time, for that matter. I had told him the difference between his left foot and his right foot, but I was so busy resenting the intrusions in my carefully planned schedule that it had never dawned on me to tell him about God.

There are dozens of Franks and Lindseys in my neighborhood, and I can't say I'm always delighted when three or four arrive at the same time. But when I start feeling sorry for myself and wishing their parents would take more turns, I remember Frank's "Thanks." Because of these children, I have many opportunities to do God's work, and sometimes that means slathering peanut butter on Lindsey's slice of whole wheat.

This is not to say you shouldn't set rules in your own home regarding appropriate playtimes and behaviors. If word gets around that "anything goes" at your house, it won't be long before your welcome mat turns you into a doormat, and that's not good stewardship of your time and resources. Nevertheless, Frank and Lindsey taught me that it's a good idea to develop a bit more flexibility when entertaining young (and sometimes uninvited) guests.

When the noise and fingerprints get on my nerves, it's good to remember: I may be the only person in this child's life for whom "God" is not a swear word. Will my love for the Heavenly Father translate into love for this precious little stranger, for whom God's child gave His life?

What's the "Job" of a Modern Mother?

A friend told me about a young mother who really has a heart for ministry. She spends hours a week preparing for an organized Bible study, participates in countless church projects, and volunteers to bake, baby-sit, decorate for luncheons, and take meals to the sick.

Despite all that, she feels guilty because she wonders if she ought to be involved in a new witnessing program. The problem is, she's totally exhausted. She wants so much to serve the Lord, but sometimes it's hard to work in yet another ministry when you have, as she does, three preschoolers.

Sound familiar? I wish I could gather all the Wonder Women of the world in my kitchen and share the good news: If you are mothering little children, that *is* your ministry. Whether or not you work outside your home, caring for those precious lives is the ministry to which God has called you and the career for which He is more than willing to train you.

In fact, Jesus said, "Anyone who takes care of a little child like this is caring for me! And whoever cares for me is caring for God who sent me. Your care for others is the measure of your greatness" (Luke 9:48, TLB).

Christian Women Are to Disciple Young Believers

If you doubt the importance or potential impact of your work, consider how many encounters with lost souls each of your children will have in a lifetime. Multiply their influence over and over, and in your mind's eye see it carrying on long after you (even they) have left this world.

As a Christian, should you look for opportunities to disciple young believers? Absolutely. And what better place to begin than in your own kitchen, or kneeling beside your child's bed, praying *with* him or her when he or she is awake and praying *for* your child when he or she is asleep?

Why do we mothers sometimes feel we must wear ourselves out participating in a variety of ministries—when our most important ministry is under our own roof? Carve a chunk out of your schedule for Bible study and prayer, and if you have time left over in which to help out in other worthy causes, great. If not, take off six months or a year, then reevaluate. No job, project, or committee can possibly be more important than the families with which God has entrusted us, and spending time in His Word and in His presence is what equips us for the task.

Blowing Bubbles Can Be God's Work

One hectic afternoon (come to think of it, they were *all* hectic) when Lauren was a toddler, she came waddling toward me at full speed, clutching a yellow plastic bottle as if it contained the gold of a thousand kings. "Blow bubbles," she pleaded. "Outside."

Oh, no. Another interruption, and the day was already packed with obligations. In an instant I could think of half a dozen reasons to snuff out the flicker of hope in her eyes. I had to start dinner. The den looked like a motorcycle gang had met there for lunch. I needed to call the bank and stop payment on a check. It was too cold outside. She wasn't even dressed yet, and it was two o'clock. Besides, she always—*always*—knocked the bottle over and made a mess.

No, it was a bad day to blow bubbles; but as I began

to tell her so, the words caught like tiny barbed anchors in my throat. "OK," came the mommy verdict, "but first you'll have to get some clothes on. Then we'll go outside for a little while."

With amazing speed she scooted up the stairs, let me pull a shirt over her head without the usual wrestling match, held her legs still while I slipped on her overalls, and helped with her socks and shoes. In a matter of minutes we were on the porch step, and I was struggling to open the childproof cap on a jumbo-size bottle of bubbles.

It was a warm day, much warmer than I had thought. The sun was bright without being harsh, and a slight breeze stirred the leaves, some of them already crisping in the first days of fall. I pulled a blue wand out of the bottle and puffed gently. Dozens of bubbles fluttered like newly hatched butterflies and drifted over our heads, casting off rainbows while they spun.

"Let me do it!" she said. Her lips puckered, she blew at the wand, and after several tries she did manage to release one bubble, then another and another. One floated into the rosebush, another to the peak in the roof. Yet another perched a moment on a blanket of phlox, then exploded like a silent sneeze. She smiled, and in her eyes I saw more rainbows.

Before long she was chasing a daddy longlegs into a crack in the porch, then running circles around the maple tree and turning a somersault in the grass. In the process she managed to knock over the bottle and spill half the soap—I knew it!—on the sidewalk. We hosed it down and watered the potted geraniums while we were at it, and she gave the living room window a shot before I could grab the hose.

When I said it was time to go inside, she agreed, because she wanted to help prepare supper. What she did was rearrange the kitchen cabinets while I threw together a tuna casserole.

Come suppertime, nobody was very hungry, and I decided the casserole was a waste of time. The den was still a mess, but it took only a second to sweep the puzzle pieces into a pile and a couple more seconds to shove the magazines into the rack and the books onto the bookshelf. I put the phone call on my list of things to do the next day. Or the next.

I picked up a yellow bottle of bubbles, half empty, and set it on the shelf to await another warm fall afternoon. Suddenly I realized that all my reasons as to why it was not a good day for blowing bubbles had vanished into thin air, just like the bubbles that shed rainbows and then melted into the sky.

It is never a bad day to blow bubbles with a child. It had been so long since I was two—and oh-so-in-love with simple miracles—that I had forgotten.

Many things that the business world considers important happened that day. Corporations merged, lawsuits were settled, stocks rose and fell, some companies were started, and others went bankrupt. Eventually, every one of those things will be insignificant and forgotten. But the minutes I spent investing in the life of one child will matter forever. *That's* what it means to be a mother.

Want to do something for Jesus today? Take a toddler to the park. Blow bubbles. Gather up some gardening tools and play in the dirt. Make Kool-Aid. Read *The Cat in the Hat* 47 times. And rest assured: When you do these things, you are doing God's work.

I have a new day planner, and in weeks when I'm organized enough actually to use it, it's a handy tool. But over time I've learned to appreciate interruptions—interruptions that sometimes mean that nothing on my to-do list gets done.

Some of those interruptions take the form of a child who needs attention. Some of them I bring on myself because of poor planning (or failing to supervise an ill-behaved house pet). In either case, when things don't go according to my carefully laid plans, it helps to adjust my focus and zoom in on the Father instead of the problem. His pillows are everywhere. I'm still learning what a relief it is to fall back onto them and relax.

Bottom Line

Think about some of the interruptions God has allowed into your life in the past 24 hours. Which of them might have been pillows, redirecting you to a place He wanted you to be?

Interruptions

1.

2.

3.

4.

5.

4

Getting Along with a Difficult Coworker (The One I Married)

WE ARE COMPLETELY INCOMPATIBLE. I TOOK VIOLIN LESSONS; he took karate. He likes five-speeds; I can't drive anything without an automatic transmission. He works the *New York Times* crossword puzzle with an ink pen; I change my mind so often I have to do my grocery list in pencil.

On the matter of shoes, he thinks 20 pair are sufficient for four people. I think that's a minimum for one busy woman. I own many more than he does, he says, as if he's making a relevant point. I say he owns more crescent wrenches than I do, so what does that prove?

On our first date he took me home at 10 P.M., because his hockey team had a game at 11 and he didn't want to be late. I not only couldn't skate but knew next to nothing about hockey, until he took me to a game (second date). I still don't understand what they're doing out there on the ice, but I clap a lot—to keep warm.

He can't stand onions; I think every dinner worth eating begins with an onion gently sauteed in a nonstick pan. He balances his credit union checkbook to the penny every month, and I maintain two checking accounts in separate banks, so that when one is impossibly messed up, I can switch to the other account for six months, allowing plenty of time for the numbers to even up on their own. Worst of all, he's an engineer.

Being married to an engineer means trudging to the mailbox hoping for *Better Homes and Gardens* and lugging back *Automotive News, Ward's Auto World,* and *Road and Track.* It means finding "tachometer" at the top of a Christmas list and sitting in the den on Thanksgiving watching a videotaped replay of the previous year's Indianapolis 500.

Engineers don't understand why other people can't take apart a busted coffeepot or Boeing 747 and put it together again so that it works, and they cannot resist the impulse to explain how they fixed it: "Look—it's easy," they'll say, wire strippers in one hand, a wad of multicolored, spaghetti-tangled cords in the other, and a diagram that looks like the blueprint for a space shuttle spread on the kitchen counter.

We've been married 13 years now and still haven't agreed on a china pattern. Before the wedding all I could think to register for was brown bath towels and *The Joy of Cooking.* Consequently, we have enough towels to mop up an oil slick but are no closer to dining elegantly than we were during the Carter administration. Coming to an agreement on something as major as china is going to require a summit conference.

Those of you in incompatible relationships know what I mean. I want pretty dishes. Not necessarily the pattern with the fruit basket that costs five zillion bucks a place setting, but something with a tasteful border of pastel flowers would be nice. The ones I like have dainty and charming names: Charleston, Mount Vernon, Rose Manor.

The engineer wants geometric. No flowers or swirly stuff. Just rectangles and a few bold lines on a soup bowl the size of a hubcap. He'd be thrilled if Lenox came out with a pattern in steel gray called "Crankshaft" or "Moonlight over Detroit."

Compatible? Hardly at all. I wanted to spend our wedding money on something wildly romantic, like a resort hotel where you can stand knee-deep in the ocean and still see your feet. We bought a computer instead.

His hobby is repairing broken appliances; mine is sneaking them into the trash while he's at work.

When it comes to compatibility versus incompatibility, you can file this under odd but true: The very traits that attract us to our mates in the first place, we later find annoying.

For example, when my husband and I began dating, I thought it was great that he took an entire Saturday to replace the exhaust system on my car. Now it drives me crazy when I can't find space in the garage for gardening supplies, because he has so many tools.

When we were first married I was thrilled that he didn't expect a three-course dinner on the table every night, because I didn't get home from work until 6 or 7 P.M., and I was too tired to do anything but open a can of Spaghetti-O's or microwave a frozen pizza. The down side is that now when I do put myself out and whip up a pot roast with mashed potatoes and gravy, he doesn't seem to appreciate it as much as I'd like.

See what happens? Over time, I have a tendency to overlook the positive side of my mate's characteristics and dwell instead on the negative. When that happens, I need to go back to something I memorized years ago, long before I even imagined these words might apply to a future husband: "Finally, brethren, whatsoever things are true, whatsoever things are honest, whatsoever things are just, whatsoever things are pure, whatsoever things are lovely, whatsoever things are of good report; if there be any virtue, and if there be any praise, think on these things" (Phil. 4:8, KJV).

When I break those guidelines down into bite-sized chunks and apply them to my spouse and his sometimes annoying habits, what a difference it makes!

✼ Yes, he leaves his cereal bowl in the sink instead of putting it in the dishwasher, but I can always count on him to tell me the truth.

✼ Yes, his channel surfing when I'm trying to watch TV drives me crazy, but he's honorable in his business dealings.

✼ Yes, he stacks papers and magazines on the bedroom floor, making it difficult to vacuum, but he's always fair when we have a disagreement regarding finances or child rearing.

✼ Yes, he forgets to clean the sink after shaving, but he's a faithful husband and a loving dad.

✼ Yes, he neglects to call and let me know he's going to be late for dinner, but while I'm chiseling the charcoal edges off a pan of lasagna, I remember how hard he works and that he wouldn't put up with the long hours if he didn't have to provide for our family.

Does he have some funny habits and annoying quirks? Sure—just like the rest of the human race. But his heart's desire is to serve God and be a good husband and father. In the long run, I guess that ought to count for more than remembering to put his socks in the hamper.

When a coworker got on my nerves at the office, I always found relief in the knowledge that eventually he or she would be transferred or promoted out of my life. When the man I married—my coworker for life—gets on my nerves, that isn't an option. That's why my thinking needs to change, whether or not his behaviors ever do.

Filing a Grievance on the Home Front

Birthdays come and go, and most of the time there's no reason to make a big deal over them. I felt this way especially about my husband's birthday—the year he forgot *mine*.

Actually, he'll deny that he forgot. He had planned to stop by a store after work and buy a nice present, but he had to stay late at the office. By the time he got to the store it was closed, so he came home empty-handed.

I could not believe it. All that time and money wasted in marriage enrichment seminars. All those painstaking explanations of how much I like gifts wrapped in floral print papers and tied with coordinating ribbons, and Hallmark greeting cards. There it was my birthday, and he didn't even stop at the supermarket for a fistful of carnations. Forget the cards and the fancy wrapping paper—that late in the day I would gladly have taken cash.

Really, now. Even if you don't think birthdays are that special, if you know that your own true love considers them slightly more important than the gross national products of entire continents, wouldn't common sense tell you to play along? Detecting my depression, he did go out into the night to scavenge flowers, a cake, and a greeting card from a 24-hour shopping mart. He should have quit while he was only neck deep in trouble, but in a desperate attempt to save himself, he mentioned a refund I had coming on wallpaper.

Why didn't I, he wondered, use the cash to buy myself a present?

That disastrous birthday was in June. Then, just a couple of weeks before his November birthday, he mentioned that he would like an IBM-compatible computer chess game and a golf glove. He had a lot of nerve, I said, giving me a birthday list, *under the circumstances.*

What circumstances? he wondered. Some men never learn.

I told him when the big day came I would take him to dinner. I love going out to dinner, and he doesn't care much about eating at restaurants, so I figured it was the perfect way to celebrate his birthday.

As we were eating at a Red Lobster (he's not crazy about fish, so that's where I took him), he said a coworker had asked if he had anything special planned that night. "Nothing," he told her, "except my wife is taking me out to dinner. And I think she's giving me a surprise party."

"Why?" asked the coworker.

"Because she cleaned house. And she cleans house only when we're having company."

We laughed about the story. I mean, not only was it insulting—imagine that, broadcasting my slovenly housekeeping habits—but how could he possibly think I would go to that much trouble after that terrible, terrible day in June?

You think you know someone. You take walks in the woods, argue about politics and Scrabble rules and how to discipline children. You enjoy your shared interests, study your differences, and come to a few compromises along the way. All things considered, we work these things out pretty well, and if the truth be told (don't tell *him* I said this), I like buying my own presents. It's the only way I get exactly what I want, and it always fits.

I would have laughed even harder and longer at that absurd observation about my housekeeping, but there were 15 people back home grinding potato chips into a freshly vacuumed carpet, waiting to jump out of the dark and surprise him.

The Pros Tell How to Get Along

If you're in the habit of forgiving your partner for small disappointments, it will be easier to forgive when a big one comes along.

A few years ago I asked readers of my newspaper column for the secrets of happy marriages. I hadn't been married very long myself, and it sounded like a good way to get free advice from the pros.

I'll always remember this note from a woman married 49 and one-half years:

> Nothing comes easy, especially a marriage. Why do we overlook slights, hurts, sarcasm, even double-crossing in the business world, but let it come to a marriage partner, and both parties are ready to give up? Anything worth having is surely worth working to keep, improve, and enjoy. I never did believe marriage was 50-50. More like 90-10. But sometimes the 90 is yours, the next time your husband's.

For those of us married a relatively short time, it's hard to imagine those silver and golden anniversaries. One woman, married 34 years, offered this peek into the future:

> [My husband and I] believe the basic ingredients in our marriage, besides simply loving one another, are kindness, consideration, a willingness to admit being wrong, humor, and the willingness to endure each other's faults.
>
> As hair and teeth fall out, wrinkles creep in, and bulges appear in the wrong places, we continue to look at each other with love and tenderness. With myopic eyes, we see only the young girl and the boy who vowed to love one another forever.

In analyzing nearly 100 replies from men and women who wrote about their long (and usually happy) marriages, four qualities kept turning up: love, giving, faith, and commitment.

Those marriages are not necessarily without sadness, as evidenced by this reply from a couple married 35 years. Asked their secret, they replied:

> A lot of love and respect for each other, the ability

to laugh with, but not at, each other, and a tremendous pride in our children.

We've shared our successes and our grief (we lost one son to cancer). Our church and our faith have been and still are an integral part of all our lives. We've never found—or looked for—any better criteria for daily living than the Ten Commandments and the Golden Rule. A good marriage is worth all the effort that has to go into it every day.

If you take a close look at the marriages represented over the years in your circle of relatives, friends, and acquaintances, you'll observe some that crumbled because of seemingly minor disagreements and others that survived against tremendous odds. What makes the difference?

When Marriage Goes from Better to Worse

When they got married back in the '50s, they rattled off "for better or for worse, in sickness and in health" automatically, with scarcely a thought, because the words were so familiar, and they were, after all, anxious to get on with the honeymoon.

She was a teacher, he was a foreman, and they lived in a pretty house overlooking the water. In the early years of their marriage they had five children, one right after the other, so it's understandable that they sometimes argued. That frightened the kids, because they thought it meant Mom and Dad didn't love each other, but Mom and Dad insisted they did.

Then something started to go very wrong. She started feeling sick all the time and couldn't finish the projects she started. She kept getting worse, and it took 10 years before the doctors—and there were dozens—decided that her muscles were deteriorating.

Some patients with her illness live relatively normal lives for decades, but in her case the disease led to paralysis and an inability to communicate the thoughts raging like bound cats inside her head. She could not turn the dial to choose her own radio programs, or feed herself, or file her nails, or comb her hair. She lay in bed all day and all night on her left side until someone rolled her onto her right.

Her husband paid a neighbor to look after her during the day while he was at work, but on evenings and weekends he took over. He fed her little bits of chicken and egg and tried to tempt her with chocolate cake. He told her how his day had gone and stroked her hands and curled fingers.

"The doctor is coming to check on Mom this evening," he told the kids one hot afternoon. The doctor had not been there in more than a year. There was no need, because there had been no change for the better and no change for the worse.

When the doctor left that night, he carried his bag and the burden that falls on medical people when they are faced with diseases that magnify their helplessness.

"He says she's doing fine," said the husband. The corners of his mouth turned up as though he might laugh at the irony of that, but he walked into the kitchen for a drink of water instead.

I didn't have the courage, but I wanted to ask him why he did it, why he kept her at home, spent his money looking for cures, and most of all, why he was there when so many others under similar circumstances choose to flee. I lacked the nerve, but if I had asked and he had the words, I think he would have responded, "Because I love her, and because I promised I would."

Prescription for an Ailing Marriage

You can leave a job you don't like when things go wrong. When you have a personality clash or disagreement with a coworker, you can look forward to the day when one of you will move on. But marriage is a lifetime commitment, for better or worse. With that understood, wouldn't it be wise for us to do our best to make it *better?*

A while back I heard Howard Hendricks, author, speaker, and staff member at Dallas Theological Seminary, suggest an exercise that can be a healing prescription in a troubled marriage and a delightful bonus in a marriage that is already strong. It couldn't be simpler—or more profound: *Make a list of the things you like about your mate.*

When I do that, the engineer's annoying habits somehow become transformed into more positive qualities. True, his toolboxes sometimes get in my way, but the power mower in the garage cost $5.00 and didn't work when my engineer bought it; now it could mow Iowa.

With minimal tinkering and trips to the hardware and electronics stores, he's also repaired a coffeepot, two hair dryers, the washing machine, a crooked floor lamp, assorted television sets, and the window, horn, and dome light on my car. One day I came home from the supermarket to find that he'd wired the living room, den, and basement for stereo. I figure that with all the money we've saved, I can feel free to stock up on another 20 pair of shoes (a calculation that will undoubtedly bring him less joy than it does me).

As I think about it, the list grows longer. He listens when I give advice, he's good with the kids, he encourages me in new interests, he welcomes visits from my parents and other relatives, he gives me first chance at the Sunday crossword puzzle—well, you get the idea.

Bottom Line

Refresh your memory. What are the things you like about your mate? Some of us can fill a notebook; others will struggle to come up with 10. In either case, it's worth the effort.

1.

2.

3.

4.

5.

6.

7.

8.

9.

10.

5

You Can Blame the Bottom Line on Toilet Fairies

THE EARLIEST SIGN OF TROUBLE IN MY MARRIAGE WAS THE POSItion of the toilet seat.

Everyone knows toilet seats should be left *down*, and it's the pinnacle of rudeness to depart a lavatory with the seat in the *up* position. God designed an orderly universe, and that's one of the basics.

Needless to say, I was shocked to discover shortly after the honeymoon that my husband was unaware of this fact. I casually mentioned it, assuming that would take care of the problem. Then I mentioned it again—and again—and again. Then I worked just a hint of a tremble into my voice to make sure he understood the importance of my request. Still no response.

Was I not a reasonable person? On all other subjects, he offered convincing arguments to support his opinion or admitted I was right. It wasn't like him to ignore my pleas, and for the first time in my life I found tears coming to my eyes over the position of a toilet seat.

Up meant my beloved didn't care about my feelings and couldn't possibly love me as much as I'd hoped. He thought I might be blowing things out of proportion just a bit.

We were at a stalemate, with 49 years, 10 months, and two weeks to go before our golden anniversary. If we couldn't come to some sort of understanding regarding toilet seat etiquette, it was going to be a rough half century.

The Bible doesn't specifically deal with this issue, so you kind of have to read between the lines.

What would the Proverbs 31 woman do under the same circumstances? She's a woman of stamina and poise, strength and dignity, isn't she? (See Prov. 31:25.) She will help her husband and not hinder him, won't she? (See Prov. 31:12.) And she's got to be creative if she can manage all those servants, care for her family, and run a business on the side.

Creative: I like that word when it's applied to a marriage.

The more I thought about it, the more I realized it couldn't be my loving husband who was stomping all over my sensibilities. Someone else was playing a cruel trick. Someone who was trying to drive a wedge between us. Someone who thought he or she would never be found out. I couldn't wait to share the discovery.

When the mood seemed right one evening, I broke the news: "We have toilet fairies living in this house."

He stared.

"No, really. I've finally figured out what's going on, and I want you to forgive me for accusing you of something you'd never do. Those pesky toilet fairies snuck in the bathroom after you left and put the seat up. They knew you'd get blamed for it."

He still stared, but before long he started to smile. He agreed we had a problem, and neither of us knew quite what to do about it. In the hall closet we had sprays and solutions for ants, wasps, spiders, and mildew, but no label promised to rid a home of toilet fairies. I said we would most likely have to learn to live with them, and he cheerfully agreed.

Over the next few days the most amazing thing happened. The toilet fairies must have overheard the conversation and realized they'd gone too far, because they started taking fewer chances. Before long, the toilet seat was left down more times than it was left up.

They weren't totally reformed, of course. On rare occasions I discovered they were back to their old habits, and when I did I mentioned ever so casually, "The toilet fairies are at it again. They're trying to get you into trouble." He would laugh, and what might have developed into a heated discussion on the subject of unmet expectations instead turned into a gentle reminder that marriage is a lot more fun if both parties develop a sense of humor regarding their mate's "flaws."

Over time a far more important change has taken place. Finding the seat up doesn't bother me nearly so much as it used to, because I have a hard time staying mad while I'm laughing.

Fortunately, my partner feels the same way, because in all fairness I should point out that there are a few things I do that annoy him. For example, every summer he drags out the fertilizer spreader, the hoses, the mower, and the trimmer and watches for dandelions with the grim determination of a border guard. If he were on the jury, a defendant convicted of driving a car across another person's lawn would be sent directly to the electric chair.

One day when the ground was soft after several days of rain, he discovered deep tracks in the grass a few inches to the left of the driveway, pointed at the mud on the tires of my car, and rather sternly requested an explanation.

"Obviously," I replied sweetly, "the toilet fairies have learned to drive."

Fireworks on Valentine's Day

In the business world, when you have a conflict with a coworker you have several options:

✻ Ask for a transfer.

✻ Appeal to your supervisor or union representative to mediate.

✻ Invite your coworker to lunch, and try to talk things out.

If you choose the last option, often you'll find that miscommunication was at the root of the problem. That holds true in marriage as well. Ironically, one of the first crises in my relationship with my husband concerned romantic symbolism.

"I like flowers," I remarked one day, inserting a hint into the conversation as neatly—I thought—as a foot into a comfortable slipper.

"Then maybe you ought to think about growing a garden sometime," he said, missing the point entirely.

"No, I mean I like *getting* flowers. I would like you to send me flowers occasionally."

This is where the magazine articles that stress honesty and open lines of communication in a relationship skip a step. According to *them*, he was supposed to say, "Why, thank you for telling me. I wasn't aware of your feelings, and it's good to know that such a simple thing will make you happy. I'll do it gladly."

No man has ever said that. Veering from the anticipated script, he said, "What do you want dead flowers for? Flowers wilt."

A calm and reasonable discussion followed, during which I stressed the importance of symbols and told touching tales of the past, in which flowers had played significant, appreciated, and well-remembered roles.

He countered by stressing the importance of budgeting money for necessities and told touching tales of the past, in which practicality had played a significant, appreciated, and well-remembered role.

Nothing in *Mademoiselle* had prepared me for this viewpoint.

"You should realize he's got a scientific mind," said a friend who probably meant well.

Ah, yes. I know of the void between science and romance, between logic and emotion, between pocket calculators and carnations. And I think Einstein was a wonderful man—but I wouldn't want to date him.

The topic, ever simmering on the back burner, boiled over several times in the ensuing months, most dramatically when I mentioned—casually?—how much I liked the flowers someone sent my dental hygienist.

"I don't understand why my sending flowers to you is so important," he said. Again.

"You don't have to understand it in order to do it," I replied through smiling but gritted teeth. *"Please."* He said he would.

"Boy, they sure charge a lot for flowers," he reported a few days later. "I told a florist I wanted to send three roses, and she said the minimum order was $22, plus $4 for handling. Is there a cheaper way to do it?"

I was meaningfully silent, thinking that perhaps open lines of communication are overrated.

"This is not very romantic," I said finally. "I think I know romantic, and this definitely is not it."

I should have left it at that, but instead I added, "Why don't you just give me the money, and I'll shop around to see if I can get a better deal?"

He was sorry. Really sorry.

I felt lousy for making a big deal out of a romantic cliché, considering the nice things he'd been doing all along, the hours he spent under my car trying to make it run right, the funny cards, the phone calls, the gentle and caring words, the trip to the store when I ran out of cream cheese and had to have it that minute. And especially considering the nice person he is—his patience, his kindness, his humor, his sensitivity, his understanding, his forgiveness when I disappoint *him*.

"How about Valentine's Day?" he said, aiming for a truce. "I could send you flowers on Valentine's Day . . ."

I smiled.

". . . When is it?"

Tenderness and Toilet Fairies

When I think about the many areas in which my husband and I are obviously not compatible, I am reminded of Eph. 4:32, which says, "Be kind and compassionate to one another, forgiving each other, just as in Christ God forgave you." My King James Bible uses the word "tenderhearted," which is a perfect description of the relationship between husbands and wives who truly pattern their marriage after Christ's relationship with His Church.

If I cannot be tenderhearted and forgiving toward my husband in small things—and problems don't get much smaller than flowers and toilet fairies—what will happen when the major challenges come our way?

The average employee in today's corporate world will change jobs, and perhaps even careers, as many as six times. In a world in which change and transition are the norm, how can I, as a wife and mother, create stability in my workplace—the home? Particularly when my coworker (husband) isn't being cooperative? Let's look at the office model again:

✱ *Ask for a transfer.* This isn't a realistic option if you believe God's Word is true, because it prohibits a marriage partner from taking off, even if the toilet seat is *never* down.

✱ *Appeal to your supervisor or union representative to mediate.* Actually, this isn't such a bad idea. Your minister or a trusted counselor may help you improve your communication skills as a couple. Many have benefited from wise, professional advice.

✶ *Invite your coworker to lunch, and try to talk things out.* Naturally, this works only if your partner is willing to talk. Not everyone is comfortable sharing his or her deepest thoughts, fears, and concerns with another person, even a spouse. Therefore, go slow, do your research (a number of excellent books on male-female communication styles are available), and spend much time in prayer. You'll find that when we ask God to change someone else, He often finds it necessary to change us first.

Bottom Line

The next time you're tempted to blow up at your inattentive, inconsiderate, or noncommunicative spouse, take a moment to pray this prayer instead:

Dear Lord, When minor disagreements and irritations threaten to drive a wedge between my husband and me, please keep my heart tender and my mouth closed. It is because of our differences that we are stronger together than we are apart. Help me celebrate those differences as gifts from You, and let me see the humor in them.

6

All Stressed Out and No Place to Go

Arline made straight A's in high school, and her teachers let her know they thought she was nuts for not going to college. But after graduation my older sister went to work as a secretary and got married a year later.

She quit her job shortly before her first baby came along. While her husband was earning his undergraduate degree, then a master's, and finally a doctorate, she went to plenty of parties where the conversation revolved around school.

"I always felt inferior," she says. "I was intimidated. I had the mistaken idea that a person's worth was somehow connected with whether they had a college degree."

Along about the time she turned 40, that began to change. The mother of two teenage boys, she returned to the workforce after 18 years as a full-time homemaker. Was she nervous?

"Absolutely," she says. "I was scared and unsure of myself, but at the same time I was looking forward to it, because I thought the challenge of doing something new would be exciting."

The "something new" was editing an academic journal. A family friend—a professor—asked if she'd like a job. He knew she was a stickler for detail and a whiz at grammar, and so he made the offer. She liked the idea of being stretched as a person and thought getting out might be fun. Besides, with two boys to put through college, the added income was a blessing.

Still, she hadn't been in the workforce for some time and didn't feel qualified for the job. On top of her routine insecurities was added another: the transition from typewriter to computer.

She bought a stack of books billed as "user friendly," which means they were written in a language that remotely resembles English. One day the professor asked her to put something on a spreadsheet. When she said she didn't know how, he remarked, "It's easy! I taught myself in 20 minutes," and then he walked out of the room. She looked up "spreadsheet" in one of her manuals and had it figured out by the end of the day.

One by one the insecurities began melting away. She was especially worried about making corrections in articles written by experts, but as she gained confidence, it got easier.

"My office is on a university campus," she says, "and rubbing shoulders every day with professors, I've come to realize that they're just ordinary people who happen to have degrees in certain fields, and some of them don't have as much life experience and general knowledge as I do. And in terms of organization and attention to detail, I can see that I'm far ahead of most of them."

Does she regret stepping out of the paid labor force for almost two decades? Not a bit.

"I think raising children is the most important task I could have had in my entire life, and it's really not that big a chunk out of my life, if you think about it. I wanted to teach my children values that are important to me, and just the joy of being with them—I didn't want to give that up. Each day held something new, and I didn't want to miss it.

"I don't feel that I missed out on anything. I had to wait longer to get some things, like furniture and nice clothes, but the things I have now don't have 20 years of wear on them, either! I can't really think of anything that I missed out on."

Many current magazine articles focus on women who have the smarts and the ambition to "have it all," and once in a while it's refreshing to run across a woman who says you don't have to have it *all at once.*

Are you, like Arline, at a stage in your life in which you're considering the possibility of entering or reentering the paid workforce? At one time or another many of us will face that challenge. It can be a frightening and stressful prospect, particularly if you're unsure of your skills or work in an area in which technology changes rapidly. When I left my job as a newspaper reporter, there wasn't a single fax machine in the building in which I worked. Now it's practically a necessity in my *home* office.

For some, part-time work or volunteerism may be the answer to keeping up while their career is on hold. For others, a home-based business offers financial rewards, as well as the opportunity to stay up-to-date in the marketplace.

Home Is Where the Heartburn Is

Before you consider a home-based business, make sure you're aware of the potential pitfalls. A few years ago a working mother by the name of Phyllis Gillis quit a job with great benefits, started her own business, and wrote a book about the experience, titled *Entrepreneurial Mothers.*

What led to her decision? "I was so short-tempered all the time with everybody around me," Gillis told me. "I didn't like *me* very much, I was so stretched. I didn't have the energy or the strength to think about what I was going to fix for dinner. I felt in pieces, like a jigsaw puzzle scattered all over the room."[1]

Sound familiar? Unlike so many others, Gillis decided to do something about the situation. She drew on her background in writing and a lifelong interest in baking. She'd worked her way through college by helping to cater parties, so it seemed natural to use that experience in starting her own business.

After much planning, she rented time in a restaurant kitchen during off-hours and made desserts for several restaurants in her Pennsylvania community. Flexible hours enabled her to attend her son's school functions, and almost immediately she felt like a better parent.

Meanwhile, she was also researching women who had gone out on a limb and started businesses ranging from a financial counseling firm, to a carpooling service, to floral arranging. Not everyone succeeded, of course. One woman had to go back to her old job to pay her debts from a failed cookie business.

The most common mistakes, says Gillis, are undercapitalization, expectations that are too high, not enough planning, and going in over your head. Also, you need to make a very realistic assessment of what you're capable of doing. The entrepreneur needs persistence, drive, enthusiasm, and business sense to step back and cut losses when necessary. In addition, she must really believe in her idea and herself.

Knowing how to research a business, including local regulations, is imperative, and a woman's best investment of all, says Gillis, may be an hour of an accountant's time. When she was contemplating a restaurant business, she contacted an accountant specializing in that area. She said that for $35 he gave her $3,000 worth of advice, including the types of record keeping she should consider, how to get in touch with suppliers, and fundamentals of pricing.

Going into business is risky, and it's not for everyone. But if you miss the particular challenge of a business-related career, it may be a satisfactory option while you're at home with little ones. The business can be as simple or as complicated as you'd like it to be.

Consider checking with a former employer to see if there are jobs you could do at home on a contract or freelance basis. This can be a win-win situation, with the company hiring a known individual who is already trained, and the employee having the freedom to schedule her own hours around the needs of her family.

People have a number of reasons for wanting their own businesses: Power. Freedom. Money. But what matters most to many mothers is *time*. Not more hours in the day, because that's impossible, but the freedom to say, "My child needs me right now; work can wait."

Getting Organized Is the First Step (Or Maybe It's the Second Step—I Don't Know; I Lost My List)

"Go ahead and level with me," I said to clutter-control expert and author Don Aslett. "You won't hurt my feelings."

"Well, primarily the clutter is the biggest thing," he said, scrutinizing my desk, on which rested a bowling trophy, a withering cactus, and a fake mustache taped to the "in" box. "And you shouldn't eat food at your desk." He grimly tapped the dried coffee puddles on the tile beside my chair and the splashes on the wall above the wastebasket.

That lesson in organization took place 14 years ago, and I'm still struggling to clean up the mess. The message hit home, though. I'll be able to accomplish more—more for my family, more for my employers, more for myself—if I structure home, time, and office. I've been working hard at "de-junking" my life ever since.

If you're serious about a home-based business, and your spouse agrees, take a hard look at what kind of cooperation and support you'll be needing from the family. Will you need to turn the spare bedroom into an office or work space? What if there is no spare bedroom? Can you claim a corner of the basement, or the dining room table? If there's too much "stuff" in the way, then there's probably too much "stuff"—period. Give it away, sell it at a garage sale, or pack it up and stash it in the attic. Then you'll have some room in which to work, and family members and friends will be more likely to view your work as a job rather than a hobby.

Before you jump feet-first into a new career, though, make sure you have the space and time to devote to it. If your new job will require uninterrupted telephone conversations, perhaps you'll need to wait until your youngest child is in preschool or kindergarten. One of the dangers of a home-based business is that it, too, can pull you away from the children for whom you've given up a more traditional profession.

To avoid that situation, determine how many hours per week you can afford to devote to the business, and stick to that schedule. After a few weeks, reevaluate. You may increase the hours or decrease them, depending upon how you and your family adjust.

Finally, keep scrupulous records of expenses, including all business-related telephone calls, office supplies, postage, and equipment. When your business turns a profit—and that certainly is one of the goals—you'll be able to claim a portion of your costs on your tax return. It would be wise to seek professional guidance in this specialized area of the law, but don't be intimidated. More and more employees in the workforce are working from home, and there are legitimate deductions.

A Mom Throws in the Socks

I've been out of the mainstream workforce for only seven years, but already I experience qualms about returning someday. Will I be hopelessly out of date? Will the technology be beyond my grasp? When a potential employer asks, "Do you do windows?" will I realize he's talking about computers?

I plan to work from home until my daughter is ready for college. That gives me another eight years in which to fall hopelessly behind. When I hear horror stories from other parents—$25,000 tuition bills, for instance—I start to panic. But then I remember someone who did exactly what I plan to do, and it helps put things in perspective.

For 30 years this woman I know sewed her family's clothes, baked all the bread, and wiped noses—anybody's—when they ran. She was home when the kids left for school in the morning, home when they returned in the afternoon, home when they called to say they would be late for dinner.

She was something of a fixture about the place, built in like the kitchen cabinets, and they realize now that they probably took her for granted, because as they got older they found out that socks with holes, tossed into the hamper, don't automatically come out of the dryer neatly patched. They learned that TV dinners and fluffy, white store bread—things they'd considered delicacies—got old in a hurry, and that staying home sick in bed wasn't nearly as easy when there wasn't anybody to bring them Tylenol and magazines.

They had wondered what she did all day long—now they knew. She had been busy, they found, taking care of *them*, and now that they were somewhat liberated, with driver's licenses of their own, it shouldn't have come as any surprise when she announced, "I'm going to go back to school."

They thought it was cute when she froze a week's worth of sandwiches for her lunches, bought brand-new spiral notebooks in which she carefully printed her name, had her hair done, and enrolled in a typing class to brush up her skills.

She was self-conscious about her age and worried aloud that her pre-World War II college credits wouldn't count for anything. Her hands shook the first day, because she was so nervous, but she soon settled in, and by midterm young women of 18 and 19 were asking her advice on whether they should marry their boyfriends or if they should take bookkeeping or shorthand the next semester. She thrived on school, on the attention, on getting 100s on exams.

She's found a niche—*good*, thought her family, envisioning years of adult education classes in art appreciation and world history. But considering the practical nature of her classes, it seemed odd that they were shocked when she said, "I'm going to get a job."

Tens of thousands of women do it every year, but a lot of them need to work in order to pay bills. She didn't need the money—not really. She had a late-model car at her disposal and a joint checking account with a husband who encouraged her to buy the things she wanted.

She had always liked working, though. Before she married and for a couple of years before the first baby came along, she had enjoyed a career. Now that the youngest was nearly grown, she wanted to reclaim some of that sense of accomplishment, so the family put up with it, thinking the phase would pass.

It caused some silent turmoil and some not-so-silent grumbling in the family, where her role always had been cook, seamstress, grocery shopper, chauffeur, and returner of overdue library books. They knew the change would be good for her—but when you get comfortable with a person, you fight change, even growth, because you feel threatened.

When she landed the first job she applied for, they sent her off to work with the same trepidation that she must have felt sending them off to the first grade. Would she make friends? How would she cope with the pressure? Would she be happy? Would she remember her house key? Would she rather be a career woman than "Mom"?

There was no need to worry. Her skyrocketing self-esteem was as obvious and as attractive as her new clothes. I'll never forget my first call to her office and the receptionist who said, "I'm sorry—your mother is not at her desk right now. May I take a message?"

I wanted to say—but I didn't—"Yes. Please tell her that we're very, very proud of what she's doing—and that we'll manage to mend our own socks."

Why Women Work

In the noisy debate over whether or not mothers should work outside their homes, something is often overlooked, particularly in conservative circles. While money often is a factor, it isn't always the only consideration. It's assumed that mothers who can afford to stay home should, and that those who can't afford to stay home ought to budget more carefully so they can quit as soon as possible.

I'm going to risk tossing out a radical idea for your consideration. Some of us like to work because it's a rewarding and fulfilling way to use our God-given talents and abilities. When you've spent 4 or more years preparing for a career and have put in another 3 to 10 years working your way up in a profession, forfeiting it to raise children requires a huge adjustment, emotionally as well as financially. Sometimes the emotional adjustment can be the more difficult.

It's not that we don't want to devote ourselves to our children, because we do. But it would be helpful if others who share our commitment to home and family recognized that our choice involves sacrifice. Am I sorry I quit when I did? Absolutely not. But do I miss the camaraderie of other professionals and the exhilaration of meeting a deadline that seemed impossible? Yes.

Colossians 3:23 says, "Whatever you do, work at it with all your heart, as working for the Lord." That's what I tried to do as a full-time newspaper reporter, and that's what I try to do as a full-time mother. In my life there has been time for both, and I hope never to take that for granted.

Bottom Line

Prayer: *Lord, please help me have the courage to try new things. That may mean stretching and developing my God-given intellect and abilities, but I'm willing to do that. Please let my work—whether it is in the home, office, or factory—be for Your glory.*

7

My Power Suit Is Low on Batteries

THE BLUE BATHROBE IS THE MOST COMFORTABLE ARTICLE OF clothing I own. Competition is stiff, as it includes two Peanuts sweatshirts and an assortment of baggy shorts, any of which would enable me to march straight through the clown entrance at Ringling Brothers, no questions asked.

Nevertheless, the blue bathrobe is in a class by itself. It's thick, plush, friendly, and as cozy as a caterpillar's cocoon. It's what I was wearing one fine Tuesday morning while breakfasting on Grape-Nuts. There's really only one breakfast rule around our house, and that has to do with milk: Whatever goes into your *bowl* eventually has to go into *you*.

Now emptying half a bowl of milk one spoonful at a time could knock a big chunk out of a kid's or husband's morning. Consequently, I don't object when they lift their cereal bowls to chin level and drink the contents, as long as there's nobody around to report their swinelike behavior to the neighbors.

Having munched on very old Grape-Nuts (not as old

as the bathrobe, but old enough that the store wasn't supposed to sell them after last June), I contemplated the pool of milk at the bottom of the bowl and decided to take the easy way out myself, slurping it to the last drop.

Satisfied that my secret was safe, I trotted upstairs to get dressed but was making a quick phone call first when I heard the doorbell ring. Probably one of the neighborhood kids, I thought. No doubt the blue bathrobe is legendary in their circle. So I rushed back downstairs, hardly giving it a thought.

The young salesman saw me through the screen, so it was too late to hide. In one hand he was holding a spray bottle filled with a clear liquid, and in the other he held a rag.

He took one look at the robe and guessed I didn't want to step outside to see him demonstrate the cleanser he wanted me to buy. No problem. He could describe everything it could do.

"See those rust stains on the driveway?" He assured me the cleanser could get rid of them.

"I didn't know I had rust stains on the driveway," I said, thinking there was no way I was going to let him in for a look at our bathrooms.

"And these water spots on the door. It'll take them right off," he said, spraying the door and wiping a three-by-six-inch area with the cloth. Wonderful. The best way to make something really look dirty is to clean *part* of it.

"I don't worry about water spots on the door," I said smoothly.

"Do you have children?"

I nodded, wondering what mysterious force drives one to answer personal questions posed by a stranger on one's own porch.

"How old?"

When I told him, hope lit his clean-shaven face, and he shifted to the grimy fingerprint tactic.

"What do you use to remove all those fingerprints on your walls?"

Actually, when they get bad enough I just paint right over them, but I didn't think he'd believe me. Besides, what if a crime has been committed? I don't want to be the housecleaning fanatic on the evening news who wiped away the evidence.

Throughout our discussion, he had the hardest time looking me in the eye. Strange, for a salesman. Must be the bathrobe.

He promised his spray would clean oven racks and said several of my neighbors had bought the stuff, which cost roughly $38 for a year's supply. Unmoved, I said no. The blue bathrobe instills in me a certain amount of confidence and authority, sort of like the general's stars and the executive's gold American Express card.

Finally he conceded defeat and moved on. Poor kid, I thought. What a hot, miserable way to make college money! I wondered why he kept looking at me so funny. After all, when you go knocking on people's doors before noon, you shouldn't be surprised they're still in their bathrobes.

Well, a person has to face the day sooner or later, so I went back upstairs to brush my hair. One glance in the mirror explained it all. Over my lip was a thick, white line, an unmistakable mustache made of milk.

Dressing for the Office When the Office Is at Home

One very good thing came out of the blue bathrobe incident. I took a serious look at how my habits had changed since dropping out of the 8 A.M. freeway rush hour, and I didn't much care for what I saw. In my closet hung hundreds of dollars' worth of business suits and tailored dresses, sensible pumps in every shade of taupe and navy, a dozen shrunken T-shirts, some of them 20 years old, and a couple of pairs of sweatpants.

Every weekday morning I found myself gravitating to the T-shirts and sweatpants. If my preschooler was going to be fingerpainting with oatmeal, did I really want to clean up the mess wearing a wool skirt and blazer? Not a chance.

The truth hit. I owned the wrong wardrobe for my new profession of full-time mom. And by the way, since leaving the structure of a clearly defined day (breakfast at 7:30, lunch at noon, coffee break if and when the phone stopped ringing), my eating habits were out of control, and the pregnancy pounds not only weren't coming off—but were multiplying. One of the hidden hazards of motherhood is rediscovering just how good those Pepperidge Farm fish crackers are and realizing that while the baby gummed half a dozen of them to bits, you polished off the rest of the bag.

No wonder my self-esteem had taken a nosedive. I'd gone from a highly structured schedule to one that revolved around erratic nap times and trips to the pediatrician for frequent ear infections. Packing the diaper and toy bag for a trip to the supermarket took as much planning as packing for a business trip to Atlanta or New York. Who had time for a manicure? Or a long soak in a hot tub? Or the luxury of brushing one's teeth not once but twice a day? No wonder I felt lousy. I was focusing so much on caring for the baby that I wasn't caring for myself, and that needed to change.

Ten Steps to Becoming Human Again

Once I recognized the woman in the mirror as someone who had fallen apart, I knew I needed to start putting her back together. The process went something like this:

1. I moved my work clothes into the closet in the baby's room. Unlike her dad, she was too small to complain that I was taking up more than my fair share of her space. That allowed me to see clearly the extent of my stay-at-home wardrobe.

2. I determined what clothing items were missing from my new lifestyle and filled in the gaps over a period of months. I bought some jeans and a nylon jogging suit, which is the uniform of choice for mothers of preschoolers. I asked for turtlenecks for Christmas and invested in some good walking shoes, because I needed to exercise more.

3. I joined a weight-loss group that emphasized lifelong nutrition and learned to prepare better-balanced meals for the rest of the family, as well as myself.

4. I moved the exercise bike from the basement to the main floor and let the family know that I was "off duty" during the 45 minutes each evening that I planned to ride it.

5. I said yes when a friend with a toddler close to the age of my daughter suggested a baby-sitting swap once a week. Every other Thursday I dropped my daughter off with her for two hours, and on alternate Thursdays she dropped her son off with me. The children loved playing with each other, and the moms loved having a couple of hours to shop and eat lunch *alone*. That four hours of freedom a month was worth a dozen sessions of psychotherapy.

6. I made it a point to schedule dinner "dates" with my husband. Even though baby-sitting can be expensive, it's worth the investment if it enables you to concentrate on your spouse rather than on the small objects being hurled at the heads of complete strangers by your restless offspring. There have been many times we spent more on the baby-sitter than the meal, because a Taco Bell Burrito Supreme can be a feast when you're with someone you love (and when you've eaten lunch standing up at the sink

three days in a row, because you haven't gotten around to chipping the strained spinach off the kitchen table).

7. I rediscovered books as entertainment. When you're working 40 or more hours a week outside your home and contending with an hour-long commute on top of that, the last thing you want to do when you get home is read a book, which actually requires mental activity. When your children are old enough to participate in library story hours, or play in a sandbox, or make mud pies, that's the perfect time to indulge your latent love of reading.

When both of us needed to work off some stress, I took my daughter to one of those fast-food restaurants with an indoor playground, where she could jump repeatedly into a vat of plastic balls, and I could read a couple of chapters in a good mystery. (Now that many of those restaurants offer free refills on drinks, I can see myself getting through the entire book before going home.)

8. I got to know some of my neighbors. Until I was home with a baby, I had few opportunities to stop and talk. A lot of people are much more open to chatting when you're pushing a stroller, and it's a natural ice breaker. I developed new and deeper relationships with a number of people, because I made it a point to slow down, take some time, and say hello. There's a bonus hidden in this method as well: Mothers with older children can share information about the best baby-sitters, the best preschools, and the best community education classes.

9. I joined a women's Bible study. Nearly all the women had children about the age of mine, so we were going through the same things at the same time. They, too, were adjusting to a new lifestyle, as well as a new role in life. Just getting together once a week and comparing notes was a tremendous help.

10. Most importantly, I used my toddler's afternoon nap time for Bible study and prayer, instead of housework.

This is a crucial step, because many new mothers struggle not only on physical and emotional levels but also on a spiritual level. If we don't feel good about ourselves, it's hard to believe that anyone—including God—can find us worthy or lovable. We can, and should, seek God's help in this difficult area, because if we're ever to feel good about ourselves, He must be the source of our self-esteem. The only way for that to happen is for us to get to know Him better and better, and we do that by making Him a priority.

Believe me, the dust will still be there awaiting your attention tomorrow and the next day and the next. Ditto for dirty dishes and soiled laundry and unclipped coupons and unmade beds. Learn to let that stuff go (even when company's coming), and let God have at least a portion of the baby's nap time. You'll be amazed at the transformation He can work in you when you allow Him just those few minutes a day.

When I look back on the early days of my daughter's babyhood and toddlerhood, I remember them as exhausting, but I also remember them as the time in my life when I slowed down long enough to begin to see what truly mattered.

Never Judge a Mom by Her Appearance

It started out like any other Sunday afternoon. I was refusing to cook, so we found ourselves at Arby's for lunch. Having come from church, we looked pretty good—not our usual *Grapes of Wrath* fashion statement. I was in my second-best dry-clean-or-else dress, peach shoes, and coordinated peach stockings, which made me look like a Creamsicle from the knees down.

I ate a turkey sandwich, watched our child splatter ketchup on all exposed body parts, and sighed when she announced she needed to go potty. I looked at her father, who pretended not to recognize us. I could read the an-

My Power Suit Is Low on Batteries

swer in his eyes: "I changed diapers; I read *Are You My Mother?* 45,000 times; I let her drink A & W root beer in the front seat of my car, which is now a sticky brown; but I am not taking her to the men's room!"

Her visiting aunt and uncle explored their sandwiches as if they were looking for Donald Trump's wallet. Obviously they weren't about to volunteer. "OK," I said. "Let's go."

Now those of us who dedicate ourselves to the study of human psychological development—or catch Oprah a couple of times a week—are aware of the struggle between parent and child over independence. It's a constant challenge, deciding how much freedom to allow and when. Nowhere is this more apparent than in the case of the public rest room. There comes a time when a child insists on stepping into that stall alone, and the mature parent has to be willing to release her.

And I did. Then I heard the bolt on the door slide shut. This, I thought while beating down panic with both fists, could be a problem.

The sound of the locking door was soon followed by a high-pitched wail, as the captive realized that she didn't know how to get the lock unstuck. I thought about climbing over the door, but there was nothing to stand on. She was getting more and more frantic and refused to crawl underneath.

Only one solution presented itself. Frantically I searched for paper towels to lay on the floor and realized that modern technology has given us blow dryers not only for our hair but also for our hands. Couldn't even find a tissue in my purse. The drain below the door that separated me from the shrieking toddler looked like it contained something researchers grow in petri dishes and handle with thick gloves, but what choice did I have?

I parked dry-clean-or-else on the floor, scooted over

the drain and under the stall door, and was halfway to my goal—in a position quite similar to that of childbirth—when the rest room door swung open. I don't know who she was, but she took a very long look and departed as she had entered—in shocked silence.

"Please don't ever do that again," I said to my suddenly calm stallmate. She smiled like an angel and flushed.

Coffee Breaks Are Essential, Even If You Don't Drink Coffee

You gain a lot when you become a mom, but one of the things you give up is dignity. Just keep telling yourself: "Someday I will once again wear a blouse on which no one has wiped a nose, and shoes that have not been used to scoop kitty litter into mini mountain ranges. Someday I will walk through the supermarket without a tiny graham cracker handprint on my rear end." Until that day, take some time for yourself.

Kay Willis, founder of Mothers Matter, an organization designed to help mothers support and educate one another, recommends a minimum break of two hours per week. Those two hours should be a time when you don't have to respond to anyone's needs but your own.

What would you do with your two hours? Bubble bath? Manicure? Stroll through the museum? Take a swimming or pottery class? Or just sit in a coffee shop, staring into space, and making occasional entries in a journal?

If you really can't manage two hours, try starting with a coffee break. After all, what other members of the workforce think they have to iron shirts while they sip their decaf? Take some time for yourself; it was important when you had paid lunch hours, and it's even more important now.

Bottom Line

Determine what you need to do in order to devote a minimum of two hours a week to your own needs. Hire a baby-sitter or trade baby-sitting with another mom? Come to an agreement with your spouse or ask for help from a relative? Those two hours are important to everyone in the family, because when you take care of yourself, you're better equipped to take care of others.

The Custodial Staff Is on Strike, and Company's Coming

Plans. I know all about plans. My plan this week was to begin each day by compiling a list of things to accomplish. At last I was going to be organized. I was going to seize control of my schedule, my commitments, and my life. The carpets would be vacuumed, the pantry and freezer stocked, the bills paid, the guinea pig cage cleaned, last year's Christmas letters answered (finally), and a mountain of paperwork sorted and filed.

It might have happened, too, except for one minor glitch. My new neighbor, who is Japanese and struggling to adjust to this language and culture, has a houseguest. Her mother has been visiting for a month, and I just could not get it out of my mind that I should come up with some sort of memento for her to take back to Japan. Finally I decided to make her a counted cross-stitch bookmark.

I felt it didn't matter what I wrote on the card, because she wouldn't be able to read it anyway; but for some reason I ripped up the first version and carefully printed a new one, which said, "May God give you peace and happiness."

She was delighted with the bookmark, and when she came over to say thank you, I asked her inside. As we sat in my living room, trying to communicate with gestures and facial expressions and labored translations by her daughter, I learned that mine was the only American home to which she had been invited. Her hungry eyes devoured every dusty detail, the furniture, photographs, vases, wallpaper patterns, even the ceramic rose candlestick holders that were—you guessed it—made in Japan.

Seeing her fascination and imagining how much she wanted to share this view of authentic American life with her friends back home, I asked her daughter if she would like to come back later in the week and take pictures.

"She says yes!" said the daughter, laughing.

And so I spent an evening and part of the next day in a frantic clean-up-the-clutter campaign. Instead of sorting through papers, I shoved them under beds. The pantry is still empty, the Christmas cards unanswered, and the house in its usual state of confusion. So much for the list. Maybe another time.

Nevertheless, when my neighbor's mother left for home, she carried with her a bookmark; snapshots of my living room, bedroom, dining room, and den; and one small note to remind her that someone in America is asking God to bless her. I was wrong about her not being able to understand. Sixty years ago she studied English in school, and while she cannot speak it, her daughter explained, she *can* read it.

God's Word says, "'For I know the plans I have for you,' declares the LORD, 'plans to prosper you and not to harm you, plans to give you hope and a future'" (Jer. 29:11). As usual, my plans were not the Lord's plans.

There's much to be said for getting one's life in order, but we need to be flexible enough that we can welcome the interruptions God sends our way.

I can almost picture in my mind the Lord looking at my to-do list, smiling, and saying gently, "That's very good, dear one. But I have a better idea."

Don't Love Anything That Can't Love You Back

In an earlier chapter I mentioned Don Aslett, a man who has become famous cleaning up other people's messes. When I interviewed him several years ago for a newspaper article on his book *Is There Life After Housework?* he said something that forever changed my outlook on my own home: "To be house-proud is stupid. I don't believe in loving things that can't love you back."

Has ever a wiser word been spoken to a mother whose house is overrun and routinely ransacked by one or more preschoolers? When I went to the office every day, I was fairly certain that when I came home the house would be in pretty much the same shape as when I left. And, with the exception of one small house fire, I was right.

Stay-at-home mothers have no such assurance. On typical days it feels as if we've put in a hard 12 hours just to keep the living room from turning into a landfill comprised of Happy Meal toys, discarded clothing items, and sales flyers that we won't get around to reading until after they've expired.

If that's your situation right now, there are three basic approaches to the problem that might help you maintain your sanity. The first, and obviously the most tempting, is to hire someone to do the housework for you. The problem with a cleaning service (besides the fact that you have to pay for it) is that most of us would exhaust ourselves cleaning the house before they got there, to avoid the humiliation of them finding out how we live.

The second method is to establish a filing system in which you prioritize chores, assign times to perform them, purchase and organize professional cleaning tools and supplies, and work clockwise around each room. This system was popularized by Pam Young and Peggy Jones, the very entertaining Sidetracked Sisters whose books on the subject have by this time presumably made them so much money that they can fall back on method one.

The third method won't win you the Good Housekeeping Seal of Approval, but it may bring your stress quotient down to a manageable level. I call it the "Cheerful Apology Method." When someone happens to drop by, you say, "Sorry the house is such a mess!" and then serve refreshments. People seldom care what shape your house is in (the worse the better, because they can feel superior). But they'll remember if you were gracious, offered something to eat and drink, and took time to chat.

With this method, does it matter if you vacuum under your couch? Women who subscribe to the Cheerful Apology Method never waste effort on work that doesn't show. We shave our legs only as high as our shortest skirt, repair sagging hemlines with strapping tape, and throw afghans over the furniture when it gets dirty. Amazingly, we get away with it.

The only valid reason to vacuum under a couch is if your rich uncle sat on it and you think you might find some money that fell out of his pockets. In fact, though you'll probably never hear it mentioned in a sermon, one of the most prominent instances of sloppy housekeeping mentioned in the Bible has to do with lost money. It's found in Luke 15:8-10, and it goes like this:

> Suppose a woman has ten silver coins and loses one. Does she not light a lamp, sweep the house and search carefully until she finds it? And when she finds it, she calls her friends and neighbors together and says, "Rejoice with me; I have found my lost coin."

Jesus told that story, or parable, and if He'd left it at that, some members of the audience might have thought the emphasis was on the importance of keeping a tidier house. But he went on to say:

> In the same way, I tell you, there is rejoicing in the presence of the angels of God over one sinner who repents.

Are you wearing yourself out in order to keep the house immaculate and therefore lack the time and energy to pursue things that are more important? I can't recall my mother vacuuming all that often; but I clearly remember her sitting down with me every afternoon, until I was well into my teens, to read a Bible story or help me study for a Bible quizzing competition in which I participated.

Do the angels rejoice because you've finally managed to conquer that mildew problem in the shower? Or do they rejoice when those little ones in your care ask to hear about Jonah and the whale "one more time"?

You Can't See Life Through a Clean Window

Of all household tasks, washing windows has to be among the most pointless. All it takes is one rainstorm or a kid with a water pistol, and your work is down the drain. So why bother? I'm tempted to post a sign on Halloween that says, "Go ahead—soap the windows. Make my mother happy."

Fortunately I have a friend who does not do windows either, so ours is the Anti-Window Washers of Planet Earth Support Group. Membership is open. No dues. Call us the next time you find yourself reaching for a squeegee, and we'll talk you out of it.

There is a homemaker's trap that for me is symbolized by window washing. It is the trap of staying so busy doing chores that one never has time or energy to do anything of lasting value. After all, it's much easier to wash a window than to read a challenging magazine article or visit a widow. It's faster to wash a window than to help your children bake a cake and deliver it to a shut-in. It's less painful to wash a window than to listen to someone else's troubles when you already have enough of your own.

I find I have a tendency to use housecleaning as an excuse not to do the things I know I should. If I'm scrubbing a bathtub, I don't have to feel guilty about not writing a letter; if I'm polishing a candlestick, I can forget the women I know who could really use an afternoon of free baby-sitting; if I'm sewing a button back onto a shirt my daughter has already outgrown, I can postpone—for yet another day—the phone call to the friend who seems to talk endlessly, hears nothing I say, but always feels better when we hang up.

As much as I hate washing windows, it would be easier than the tasks that require me to minister to the needs of those around me. When I find myself in a cleaning frenzy—and that happens like clockwork at least twice a decade—I have to remind myself to ask this uncomfortable question: Of what use is a spotless house if the heart is empty?

Beating Back Busywork

Trust me—in the long run, dirt will have the last laugh. Scientific fact: No matter what you do to dirt, you're only rearranging it; *you can't get rid of it.* That's why focusing too much attention on housecleaning is the ultimate in busywork.

Many of us have worked for supervisors who drove us absolutely nuts by wasting hours of our time on meaningless and repetitive chores. A perfectly good letter had to be retyped; a perfectly good report had to be reorganized; a perfectly good story had to be rewritten; a perfectly good plan had to be scrapped. Why couldn't the boss see, we wondered, that those time-wasting, energy-devouring assignments were keeping us from accomplishing something even more important, something that would benefit both the customer and the company?

I've been caught in that frustrating circumstance countless times, yet now that I'm my own supervisor I find myself falling into the same trap. The really depressing thing is that you can't complain to the boss when *you're* the boss.

It took me awhile, but I finally figured out some things. First of all, never believe advertisements regarding cleaning products. *They* don't clean anything—*you* do. The most ludicrous example I've ever seen was an ad for an "energy saver" mop. There is no such thing. If you want to conserve energy, buy a garage door opener or a dog that can fetch—but a mop?

Second, there are simple solutions to almost any household chore. Worried that your dusty furniture won't pass the white glove test? Wear brown gloves.

Am I advocating filthy squalor and a disease-breeding lifestyle? While some relatives might argue the point, I have to say *of course not*. I just think we're too hung up on the wrong things when we can't invite a neighbor over for coffee because the dishes aren't done. Or we can't take the kids skating, because we have to get the floor stripped.

The world is full of beautiful sunsets, flowering bushes, cool breezes, birds in flight, unrushed moments waiting to be filled by loved ones, and people who need to be loved. The years you have to spend with your family are few. Children are small for such a short time, and waxy buildup will still be there when you're a great-grandmother. *Better go skating today.*

Bottom Line

Prayer: *Lord, please help me remember that when people get in the way of my plans, it may be **my plans** that need changing. And when chores get in the way of people, I need to step back and take a long look at what will last forever.*

Think about your schedule and your goals for tomorrow, and prioritize them. Consider which items on the agenda have to do with temporary household chores and which have to do with an individual who is of utmost value in the eyes of God. Are there any items that need to be rearranged?

Household Goals

1. _____
2. _____
3. _____
4. _____

People Goals

1. _____
2. _____
3. _____
4. _____

9

Please Hold My Calls—
Someone Just
Smeared Vaseline Over the
Electrical Outlet

On a snowy Lenten Sunday in March, it was my turn to stand at the front of the church to greet visitors and answer questions regarding Sunday School classes, membership, and other things of that nature. It's a large church, with close to 2,000 members, so someone needs to be available for such a task.

While the organist played a lovely postlude, my husband retrieved our daughter from junior choir. He brought her down front to wait, and she squirmed while he worked a crossword puzzle in the Sunday School paper.

"I'm hungry, Mommy," she complained in that whiny voice typical of grade-schoolers and indicted public officials. "When are we going to eat?"

"In just a few minutes," I promised and resumed the

assignment of looking friendly and approachable. Before long she was engrossed in coloring a picture, and since the crowd had dwindled to less than 200 and no one was coming my way, I decided we could leave.

"Come on—let's go," I said, slipping into my coat. She didn't move.

"Get your coat on, Sweetheart. We can leave now," I urged.

Still no response.

"I thought you were hungry," I said in a firmer, louder voice. "Aren't you anxious to get some *food?*"

She jerked to attention, gathered her belongings, and was a quarter of the way down the aisle, struggling into her jacket and dodging stragglers, as she shouted back across rows and rows and rows of pews, "Mommy, you really know how to motivate a person when you use the *F* word!"

Heads turned. Eyes widened. Mouths dropped. So, most likely, did a few Bibles. Of course, no one had heard me prodding her with the actual word *food*.

It is a kind, warm, understanding congregation with which we worship, and there were tentative—though curious—smiles as I made my way to the exit, instinctively covering the name tag on my lapel.

My husband had mysteriously vanished, so under the circumstances there really was only one reasonable response. I directed it toward a galaxy of mystified faces, most of them—thankfully—strangers to me.

"Has anyone," I asked sweetly, "seen that child's mother?"

Baby on Board: Alert the National Guard

News flash: Parenthood is physically and emotionally exhausting.

It's not usually a major crisis that wears us down, it's

the dozens upon dozens of daily challenges and little disasters that pile up and sap our energy. Did I say "energy"? That's the thing you used to have back in the days when you could put your feet up for 15 minutes on a Sunday afternoon and rest your eyes, without fear that your toddler would scale a five-foot dresser, open a jar of Vaseline, and fully cover with goo one-third of a bedroom wall—including light switch, electrical outlets, and framed pictures.

That particular grease-based finger painting project cost in the neighborhood of $200 plus a week of my time, since the wallpaper had to be stripped and the wall sanded and repainted.

No doubt about it—kids are hazardous to your health. They should come home from the hospital stamped with a message from the surgeon general—"Warning: You think smoking is dangerous? Try going out in public with a two-year-old!"

A few years ago "Baby on Board" signs were popular car accessories, and most people assumed they were gentle reminders to drive carefully because a frail little member of society needed to be protected.

Actually, they were a public service, intended to warn other drivers that there was a child in the car, and thus they should stay as far away as possible for their own safety—not the baby's. The next time you see an infant seat in the car next to you, steer clear and watch for the following:

Swift lane changes without signaling. This is a reflex action that occurs when the driver feels a pool of something oozing along the seat and through his or her pants. It is evidence of a tipped bottle or cup, previously undetected, and may involve milk, which will require dry cleaning all clothes and scrubbing the upholstery; or grape juice, which will require trading in the car at a substantial loss. In any case, the driver will be weeping.

Repeatedly drifting onto the shoulder, then jerking

back onto the freeway. Back off fast. The baby is in the backseat screaming for animal crackers, and the driver is trying to steer with one hand while groping in the bottom of the diaper bag. When she locates the crackers she'll have to rotate her shoulder socket so as to reach around back and hit a moving target (baby's mouth), all without taking her eyes off the road.

Car sidesweeping mailboxes. This signals a visibility problem, which makes sense in a vehicle with windows smeared with saliva-saturated Cheerios.

Failure to stop for a red light. A stuffed rabbit has rolled from beneath the car seat and wedged itself under the brake pedal.

Driver steering with toes while rest of body is hanging out window. This is a clear indication that diaper fumes have reached lethal proportions. Just in case the transportation department is listening, this is a good argument for mandatory installation of oxygen masks in vehicles used for transporting babies.

No day spent in the company of a child is without challenge. In the professional world you might be able to count on a coffee break once or twice a day, but in the mothering world you schedule your next coffee break for the first day of preschool or kindergarten. No doubt about it—children are physically exhausting. Sometimes, though, the emotional exhaustion is even harder to take.

Mothers on Trial

Isn't it amazing how everyone else is an expert on disciplining *your* child? As a journalist, I accept the fact that every article I write that is destined for print will first be reviewed and edited by a minimum of two other people. In newspaper work, a copy editor reads the story to check for spelling, grammar, style, and factual errors, as well as libel. Another editor reads the story to see if it accomplishes what it's supposed to. Both are free to make changes as they see fit, and neither is obligated to seek my approval. While I may consider it "my" story, they have the prerogative to "fix" it.

As a mother, I sometimes feel surrounded by "editors" who feel compelled to "fix" my parenting. For example, have you noticed that fathers, even those who spend 10 hours a day at the office or factory, become experts on child discipline as soon as they walk through that front door?

I can't tell you how many times I've heard the words "Honey, you're too soft."

"Too soft," he says. Just because I don't believe capital punishment is an appropriate consequence for Lucky Charms ground into the den carpet.

Advice from family members I can deal with, primarily by ignoring it. When it comes from complete strangers, though, that's a different story. Every time I went out in public with my wildly exuberant preschooler, I felt as if the eyes of the World Supreme Court of Parenting were on us, with the justices eager to tabulate their ballots and broadcast via satellite, "This woman is guilty of being an imperfect mother."

And how right they were! I gave up any hope of a "Mother of the Year" trophy long ago. I'm cranky when I'm tired; I sometimes fail to follow through on threats; and—because it works—I do, in moments of desperation, bribe with candy.

If I were to compare myself to Beaver Cleaver's mother, I'd feel like a failure. But you know what? Even she made mistakes. A very wise Bible teacher once pointed out that there was only one completely perfect Parent in the history of humanity. He created a perfect home for His children, He gave them everything they needed, He loved them unconditionally—and they still rebelled.

If God's children misbehave, should we really expect

ours to be without fault? And aren't you glad that it's He, and not one of the other "experts" in line behind us at the supermarket, who is the ultimate Judge regarding the job we do as parents?

Laughter: Rx for Survival

Being a good parent is more difficult than being a good business manager, because the stakes are higher. No company on the current Fortune 500 list will be in existence 1,000 years from now, and many will be dissolved or swallowed by other companies within our lifetimes. In contrast, the work we do as mothers will last *forever.*

Excuse me. What I meant to say is that the *impact* of our work will last forever. The thought of spending eternity using a toothpick to dig congealed oatmeal out of the crack in the kitchen table is just too depressing.

The way I see it, one of my main jobs as a mom is to learn to take life's little stresses less seriously and God more seriously. I truly want to believe He meant it when He said, "As a mother comforts her child, so will I comfort you" (Isa. 66:13).

One of the most effective ways in which God comforts me is with humor. I find that if I can see the funny side of a frustrating experience, it automatically becomes less frustrating. Take this little test to see how you're doing in the "dealing with stress" department.

1. Your child crawls under the table in a less-than-immaculate restaurant. You *(a)* explain the importance of maintaining good hygiene in public places and insist your child return to his or her seat; or *(b)* tell your child that if he or she finds something tasty down there, to stuff it in his or her pocket for an afternoon snack, because you forgot to pack one.

If your answer is *a*, critics will agree you are a good

mother. If it's *b*, within five years you will have saved enough money on groceries to vacation at Disney World.

2. Your child ignores your command to stop spitting on the car window. You *(a)* firmly point out the inappropriateness of his or her behavior by using methods recommended by Dr. Spock of *Baby and Child Care* fame; or *(b)* fall back on the method recommended by *Mr.* Spock of Starship Enterprise fame and squeeze the muscle in your child's shoulder until he or she shapes up or blacks out.

If your answer is *a*, critics will agree you are a good mother. If it's *b*, other mothers will seek you out and ask you to teach seminars.

3. A simple trip to the supermarket for milk turns into a disaster when your child throws a tantrum because you won't buy candy at the checkout. You *(a)* gain control of the situation by explaining the nutritional shortcomings of Gummy Bears and offer to slice up some fruit when you get home; or *(b)* smile so onlookers will *think* you are offering to slice up fruit, while you whisper into his or her little ear the words you vowed would never leave your lips: "Stop crying right now, or I'll *give* you something to cry about!"

If your answer is *a*, critics will agree you are a good mother. If it's *b*, welcome to the club—you're human.

If we learn to laugh at those small but exhausting challenges that make up most of a mother's day—and even to value them—we'll be better prepared when more serious challenges come our way. And rest assured—they will come.

Bottom Line

Think of a recent challenge you faced as a mother. Perhaps your child embarrassed you publicly or misbehaved in a way that required discipline.

How did you respond?

How do you think God would have responded?

Take a few moments to ask for His wisdom in teaching your child.

As a professional, you may have been counseled to seek out a mentor, someone with greater knowledge and experience to advise you in your career. As a parent, God is willing and eager to be your mentor. Just ask.

10

My Prayers Are Hitting the Glass Ceiling

"COME ON—ENOUGH IS ENOUGH!" THE FRUSTRATED WOMAN scribbled on a sheet of lined notebook paper. She was a single parent, bitter, angry, and sad, and she was sick and tired of what she called my "rose-colored glasses."

As a journalist I don't often receive letters from readers complaining that my stories are too positive, but that was her complaint. "It's great that you're living such a wonderful life," she wrote, "but there are a lot of people out here with occasional insurmountable problems and regular problems who don't need to keep reading how wonderful someone else's life is going."

And so it went for a page and a half. I reached for a sheet of stationery on which to write a reply, then noticed there was no signature and no return address.

While I wasn't able to respond to her letter directly, I'd like to respond to her concerns here and now, because they're valid.

Is it wrong to focus on the lighter side of life? Is it unbiblical to look for glimmers of hope and even humor in what is, without a doubt, a grim situation? In chapter 4

I mentioned Phil. 4:8, which reads, "Finally, brothers, whatever is true, whatever is noble, whatever is right, whatever is pure, whatever is lovely, whatever is admirable—if anything is excellent or praiseworthy—think about such things."

That sounds like a healthful psychological prescription when you're having an all-round bad day, but what if the problems you face are serious, even life threatening? What about a child with birth defects or leukemia? What about an abusive spouse? Drug abuse or alcoholism? Bankruptcy? Divorce? Teen pregnancy? What about all those dreadful situations that affect members of our own families and family members of friends? How do we respond to individuals who have received the worst news they could imagine?

Just a few pages before the Philippians passage, in Rom. 12:15, we read: "Rejoice with those who rejoice; mourn with those who mourn." The word "mourn" is active and implies much more than a phone call or a sympathy card with an imprinted "Thinking of you." It requires a depth of empathy that is itself born of experience with life's difficulties.

Not one of us is immune from struggle or pain. If you have a pulse, those things go with the territory.

I would not for one moment want to imply that a woman who suspends her career in order to raise children will somehow magically be rewarded with a trouble-free life. You can read Bible stories to your children until you're blue in the face and buy every Focus on the Family book and tape in the warehouse, and it's still no guarantee that your children will buy into your belief system when they're young adults.

Kevin Leman, author of *Keeping Your Family Together When the World Is Falling Apart,* said in an interview, "The best we can do as parents is to guide children in the best way possible and then pray that they will make the right choices."[1]

And now for the kicker. What if you pray they make the right choices, and they make the wrong choices?

What if you pray for a loved one to stop drinking, and he or she doesn't?

What if you pray for a healthy child, and your baby has a handicap?

What if your prayers are hitting a glass ceiling and not even making their way to God?

What if your best friend is drifting away in a cloud of schizophrenia, you ask God to heal her, and He doesn't? That's what happened to me as a young adult, and it tested my faith in everything I'd ever been taught. It helped make me a skeptic, and I suppose that in a very real way, it led me into a profession in which skepticism is a requirement.

When the Praying Stopped

I can't remember a time as a child when I didn't believe that the Bible was true. I was in church twice on Sundays and again on Wednesday nights, and I understood that when I lied or was disobedient to my parents, that was sin, and I needed to ask God to forgive me.

I did ask—over and over and over again. Even as a grade-schooler I struggled with the question of how He could keep on forgiving me, when I knew I was going to fail again. On a day-to-day basis, I relied on my emotions to tell me if I was right with God, and since I rarely *felt* right, I experienced much doubt as to whether or not I was really "good" enough in God's eyes.

My senior year of high school was a time of intellectual and spiritual crisis. My closest friend, the young woman with whom I had shared my deepest thoughts and desires throughout the previous six years, was suffering from severe mental problems that sometimes left her suicidal.

Nothing I'd learned in all those years of sermons and Sunday School lessons had prepared me for that. Naturally, I prayed for her. But while dozens of people at Wednesday night prayer meeting offered up prayer requests, hardly anyone ever stood up to report an answer. Were all those prayers hitting the ceiling?

I had always loved reading and during this period was attracted to what I considered the brilliantly complex works of Bertrand Russell and Jean Paul Sartre. Other friends were soaking up the philosophy of Ayn Rand, and somehow the simple little stories of my childhood seemed farther and farther removed. Armed with my new interests, I became friends with a young man who was a charming agnostic. Ironically, it was he who introduced me to the writings of C. S. Lewis, a Christian apologist.

In the midst of this confusing period I began my freshman year at a Christian college, at which chapel was mandatory three times a week. I was still attending church, and I had to take a semester each of Old Testament and New Testament. The more I studied, the more I seriously began to question if Christianity was genuine or an elaborate story invented by men with great imaginations.

Now this will shock some of you, but I think it's important for parents to know that their own children may someday take a similar spiritual journey. I made a deal with God. I told Him, "I hope this is all true, but I don't want to believe it just because I heard it as a child; I want to believe it in a new and meaningful way, and in order to do that, I need to start with a blank slate."

In His mercy, I believe He allowed me to do that. I still went to church and read the Bible and sang hymns, as long as the words didn't presume a personal relationship with God. I was still, by the standards of most, a "good" person, but I knew better than anyone that being good wasn't the same as being right with God.

The following summer I was back at home and took a poetry class at the University of New Mexico. I had a very suave, sophisticated professor for this particular class—gray beard, wire-rimmed glasses, superior attitude—and for weeks he had been making disparaging remarks and jokes regarding the kinds of people who actually take their belief in God seriously.

One day as I was walking away from class, crossing the wide expanse of cement that paved the commons area, the thought came to me:

> For an intelligent person, this man spends a lot of time and energy making fun of something he insists he doesn't believe in. A smart person might make fun of someone he disagrees with or someone he dislikes, but why would he waste any ammunition firing darts at someone whom he says doesn't exist? That really doesn't make any sense.

Suddenly I realized that deep down he was *afraid* that God, Christianity, and the whole ball of wax might actually be true. He was clinging to a philosophy with no substance, because it made no personal demands on him.

In an instant I realized that I did believe in God and that everything I'd been reading and studying and learning pointed to His existence. It was a short step from that decision to the acknowledgement that He had communicated to us through the Bible, and that it was true as well.

Believing Is Not Enough

Of course, believing that God exists and that the Bible is true isn't enough. I teach a journalism class at Oakland University in Rochester, Michigan, and it's through my students' obsession with test grades that I've developed a method to illustrate the difference between believing in God and being right with God.

Imagine you're enrolled in a class, and it's the night of the final exam. The professor walks in and says, "You've heard my lectures and taken notes, and you've read the textbook. But I'm here to tell you that none of you knows enough to pass my test, because in order to pass, you have to score 100 percent. Not one student has ever passed, and none ever will."

While the students are faint from fear, the professor says one more thing. "I know you can't pass this test, but I'd like to introduce you to someone. This is my son. He knows the answer to every question on the test, and I've given him permission to take the test in your place, if you'll allow him to. All you have to do is ask."

That, basically, is the offer God is making to each of us. He knows we're not perfect, and He requires perfection. His solution to the problem is to let His Son take the test in our place. It's not enough that we believe He can pass the test. We have to give our permission for Him to take the test for us.

This is how we do that. First, we have to admit that we're not good enough on our own to pass God's test. No matter how many nice things we've done, or how many times we've been in church, it isn't enough. The Bible says "all have sinned," and there's a penalty for that. God's Word says "the wages of sin is death"—that is, spiritual death, or separation from God for all of eternity—"but the gift of God is eternal life" through His Son, Jesus (Rom. 3:23; 6:23).

Could I earn this gift through being a good person? No, if I were to earn it, it would be called a salary. Jesus is God's gift to us. His Word says, "For God so loved the world that he gave his one and only Son, that whoever believes in him shall not perish but have eternal life" (John 3:16). And, "If we confess our sins, he is faithful and just and will forgive us our sins and purify us from all unrighteousness" (1 John 1:9).

There's no greater gift than this: Jesus died in my place. If I believe that and ask God to forgive me for all the times I've disappointed Him, He will. If I say, *God, I don't want to live this way anymore—I want to turn my back on all that's wrong and follow You,* Jesus will step in and take the test for me, and God will say, "Congratulations—it's a perfect score. My Son did it again."

Prayer Changes Me, Even When Circumstances Remain

Since that moment in the New Mexico sun, when the door to my life opened and I invited God to step in, have all my questions and prayers been answered? No. My childhood friend remains mentally ill and is often institutionalized. Other friends and family members have been touched by tragedy of every kind, including alcoholism, car accidents, abuse, cancer, divorce, suicide, and even murder. God doesn't prevent us from suffering every consequence of evil in this world, but He does keep us from being overcome by the evil one.

The longer I walk with God, the more I see of His mercy and creativity. One of my greatest lessons as a mother has been learning how He uses simple childlike faith, much more than the ponderings of great philosophers and theologians, to draw people to himself.

The more time I spend with Him in prayer the more I see Him changing me, even when He does not change my circumstances as quickly as I would like.

Kids Ask the Toughest Questions

Bobby is four years old, brimming with energy, teeter-totter emotions, and questions that would stump a minivan full of Ph.D.'s.

Awhile back, Bobby's mother took him to the store with her. This in itself is a brave act, unless one's children agree to have their hands Super-Glued to their sides and their mouths sealed with duct tape. Because she knows what it means to shop with a busy four-year-old, Bobby's mom tried my favorite technique: bribery. She promised him a candy bar if he behaved himself.

On this day, though, Bobby's mom rolled her cart right into a sticky situation. She came upon a woman, a stranger with some type of handicap, who was having a hard time coming up with the money to buy something to eat. This touched Bobby's mom's heart, and she dug into her purse and gave all she could—everything down to the last dime of candy bar money. As you might expect, Bobby wasn't at all impressed with the display of generosity.

"He was sobbing over the loss, being promised a candy bar as we entered the store and not being able to have one now that we were leaving," she recalls. "I figured he was probably too young to understand."

Months later, on a crisp October morning, Bobby's mother dressed him in a new jogging suit before carting him off to preschool.

"I remarked what a lucky boy he was that we had enough money to buy nice new clothes, whereas some children's mommies and daddies might only have enough money for food and not enough to buy clothes and toys like he and his friends have."

Moms chatter away like that when we're dressing kids, because it holds their attention just long enough for us to slip on their pants and shirts without the process developing into a match worthy of world-class wrestling.

Then Bobby dropped the bomb. "Why didn't God make it so *everyone* has enough money?"

I call those times "Smucker's moments," because you feel as if an alien being has sucked all the intelligent answers out of your brain and replaced them with grape jelly. Nevertheless, Bobby's mom managed to recoup. She says, "I told him life is not fair, but that God would like people who have more to help those who don't have as much."

"Oh," Bobby said. "Like the time you gave money to that lady in the store who couldn't talk, so that she could buy food."

With tears in her eyes, Bobby's mom answered, "Yes, exactly."

She wonders what else her son has learned when she was absolutely sure he wasn't paying attention.

Prayer Is Talking to God—Honestly

Unlike a human parent, God isn't intimidated by our questions or our doubts. I love the Psalms, because so many of them are filled with outpourings from David when he was in physical danger, dreadfully mistreated by his enemies, and disappointed by those who should have loved and respected him. He was honest with God, and the Bible calls him a man after God's own heart.

Do you suppose David looked at life through rose-colored glasses? I don't think so. He lost his best friend, not to mental illness, but to war. He suffered ridicule from family members and was betrayed by his own son. He suffered a parent's worst nightmare when he prayed that his infant son would live and the child died.

No question—David knew how to mourn. But when it was time to rejoice, nobody could top his enthusiasm:

> I will praise you, O LORD, with all my heart;
> I will tell of all your wonders.
> I will be glad and rejoice in you;
> I will sing praise to your name,
>   O Most High. . . .
> The LORD is a refuge for the oppressed, a
>   stronghold in times of trouble.

> Those who know your name will trust in
> you, for you, LORD, have never forsaken
> those who seek you.
> —Ps. 9:1-2; 9-10

If you want to learn to pray, read the prayers of David. God didn't always say yes to his requests, but in spite of a difficult life filled with many disappointments as well as many joys, David trusted that God would never leave him. And he was right.

Bottom Line

When life's circumstances are crushing, it's not a bad idea to rush on over to Phil. 4:8 for a little refreshment. Take a few moments to reflect on the positive things in your life.

What's true?

What's noble?

What's right?

What's pure?

What's lovely?

What's admirable?

Begin a prayer to God by thanking Him for each of those things. I'm always amazed at what a little *gratitude* will do for my *attitude*.

11

The CEO Has a Sense of Humor

What do you buy a man with 89 Christmas notches on his belt, a man who cares nothing for clothes, paperbacks, or chocolate? Nothing seemed appropriate.

My friend Thomas Moore Brown, a retired engineer with the spirit of John Milton running in his veins, once wrote a poem in praise of the rainbows cast by a prism in his dining room window. There was my answer: I bought a heart-shaped prism strung on fishing line—a heart for love, a prism to double the rainbows and his joy.

He unwrapped the package, smiled his understanding, and the next time I saw the heart, it was dangling in the sunshine, flinging colors this way and that like an artist's palette exploding. Thomas was a widower who had lived in a tent during the Depression and later won ribbons for raising some of the prettiest chrysanthemums in the state of Michigan. When we met, he didn't have any grandchildren, and I didn't have any grandfathers, so we adopted each other.

Six weeks after he hung the heart in his window, he was scheduled to go into the hospital for cancer surgery.

The day before the operation I brought my then two-year-old over for a visit. She had a knack for cheering him up.

Generally she went straight for the refrigerator, where she'd spend a few minutes rearranging the magnets before plunging into the more serious task of consuming any milk and cherry pie left over from the Meals On Wheels delivery.

Ordinarily she would not have slowed down from the moment her feet hit the carpet until I forcibly strapped her back into the car seat. But this day was different. While Thomas and I sat side by side on the couch, for some reason she lay down across our laps and closed her eyes.

Neither of us could believe it. You might just as well command the tide to stop rolling in as to order this child to take a nap, and yet her breathing grew steady, her sighs deepened, her fingers curled and twitched.

Not wanting to awaken her, Thomas and I looked at photos taken in another century, photos of his family traveling by barge to their home in Florida. A boy of seven or eight rode a giant sea turtle on the beach. "That's me," he said, recalling a time before airplanes, before television, before world wars.

"I never had a baby fall asleep in my lap before," he said quietly, stroking the curve of my daughter's forehead with his fingers. He seemed to want the moment to last forever, so we sat for a long, long time on the sagging couch in a living room smelling of dust and medicine. He had nowhere to go, and I could think of nowhere more important.

On that afternoon, as I had so many times before, I struggled to find the words to ask if he felt ready to meet God, but in his usual, gentle way he steered the conversation to other areas, declining to answer my questions. He nodded politely when I tried to explain that God required more than being a "good" person, but I wasn't at all sure he agreed.

When would I find the right words? When would he listen?

Advancing Cancer Takes Its Toll

Nearly every Thursday afternoon for the following year, I stuffed my daughter into her car seat, pacified her with a coloring book, and drove to the nursing home where Thomas had moved following the surgery.

The cancer he had first noticed in 1941 was finally catching up with him. His nose, one eye, and much of his jaw and right cheek had been removed, and he wore a loose-fitting prosthesis quite similar to the mask in "The Phantom of the Opera." He was rapidly going blind in his remaining eye and losing the hearing in his best ear.

I continued to pray for Thomas, but each time I tried to talk with him about spiritual matters, he changed the subject. Then, just before Thanksgiving, he called with the news that, while taking a short walk in the middle of the night, he'd fallen. No real harm done, he insisted. Anxious staff members took X rays and tucked him back into bed. Nevertheless, the nurses seemed concerned that his pulse rate was way up.

"What did they *expect* would happen to my pulse?" he wondered with feigned bewilderment, "with all those young women running to me in the middle of the night?"

He had just celebrated his 91st birthday and still would not talk with me about things that really mattered.

A New Job for an Ex-Career Woman

The year Thomas spent in the nursing home was my first year of unemployment. My husband, who knew I missed the camaraderie and challenge of my former job as well as the steady income, was wise in his counsel. "Thomas is your work right now," he reminded me several times. "If you were still going into the office, would you have as much time to spend with him?"

I knew I wouldn't. But as Thomas continued to evade the most important subjects, and my prayers seemed to be hitting that same old glass ceiling, I grew discouraged. I even grew a little angry. Why was he so stubborn?

Finally, on a Thursday as he lay in bed, barely able to hear my greeting and small talk, I couldn't stand it anymore. In other instances throughout my adult life, I'd witnessed to people because I felt guilty—almost as though I wouldn't earn my "witnessing badge" unless I scored enough points.

This was different. I loved Thomas so much, that I wanted to know we'd meet again someday in heaven, where we'd continue the friendship that began here on earth. Bound and determined that he was going to hear me out, I decided it was now or never. I pulled out all the stops and literally shouted Bible verse after Bible verse into his ear. His roommate took notice. So did the staff members and other residents up and down the hall. "BEING A GOOD PERSON ISN'T ENOUGH, THOMAS! YOU HAVE TO ADMIT YOUR SIN, ASK GOD'S FORGIVENESS, AND INVITE JESUS INTO YOUR HEART. WILL YOU PLEASE DO THAT?"

He smiled but gave no indication that he understood. Meanwhile, my daughter had been pulling money out of my wallet while my back was turned and was happily stuffing it into the heating vent.

I went home discouraged, slightly embarrassed, and a whole lot poorer.

Always Be Prepared

First Peter 3:15 says, "Always be prepared to give an answer to everyone who asks you to give the reason for the hope that you have." I'd tried to do that and failed. The same verse says, "Do this with gentleness and respect," and I'd tried that too. I'd pleaded and urged and shared and finally shouted at full volume, but still nothing.

Then, just a few weeks before he died, I leaned close to his ear and asked Thomas—for perhaps the 10th time—if he had asked Jesus into his heart. Too weak to speak out loud, he murmured, "Yes."

I had shouted, the Holy Spirit had whispered, and Thomas had finally listened.

The following Christmas I slipped a heart-shaped prism onto the Christmas tree. When sunlight hit the glass just right, it splattered rainbows against the living room wall. Bright halos twinkled above the ceramic crèche with its sleeping baby.

There's a Difference Between Work and Career

Does God have a sense of humor? Every time I remember my normally timid little voice bellowing like an Old Testament prophet through the halls of that nursing home, I'm convinced of it. Every time I close my eyes and see the contents of my wallet disappearing into the bowels of that building, I remember the job God gave me that year and compare it with the job I'd left behind. When I was a reporter I shared lunches with celebrities like Joe Namath, Jim Palmer, and Phyllis George. I interviewed Dolly Parton, Lawrence Welk, Abigail (Dear Abby) Van Buren, and dozens of other sports figures and entertainment personalities who were famous for a short time then flickered into oblivion. I asked hundreds of questions and wrote hundreds of stories and got hundreds of letters from admiring readers.

But not one of those interviews came close to being as exciting and life changing as that simple little talk I had with Thomas, when I asked the most important question of all, and he said, "Yes."

Our careers matter. God gave each of us certain talents and abilities, and He expects us to use them. We may be accountants or editorial assistants or doctors or dental hygienists or pilots or teachers or homemakers or engineers, and we should do those jobs to the best of our ability. But one thing we should never do is to confuse a career with the work we were put here to do.

My career is journalism; my work is to share the good news that God promises us eternal life through His Son Jesus.

For All We Know, We Have Only Today

During the first four years I spent at a daily newspaper, five of the people I wrote about died. They ranged in age from less than 2 to more than 70. Two died suddenly and violently in accidents; one never experienced a healthy day from his birth; two knew that their bodies were waging war with killer diseases.

The first of the five to pass away was a perky atheist who spent her last days assembling scrapbooks for grandchildren, submitting to blood transfusions, and spouting opinions on the way her apartment building was managed. She had gentle words for friends who kept her supplied with homemade bread and conversation, bitter words for those whom she believed had wronged her.

I came to wonder if she poured her waning energy into straightening out tangles of paper and possessions because she thought the greater tangles involving people were hopeless.

The two who died unexpectedly were Judith Wax, who wrote a book about midlife called *Starting in the Middle,* and Olivier Chandon, a race car driver. Wax and her husband, Sheldon, a magazine editor, were on board a DC-10 that crashed on takeoff from Chicago. Olivier, who at the time was dating model Christie Brinkley, was killed when his car left a Palm Beach Gardens, Florida, track and crashed into a channel.

The baby who died had been born with multiple birth defects and was taken home by his parents, so that he could spend what little life he was allotted in the company of his brothers and sisters. The last of the five was a friend's mother, whose funeral was held on the day of her youngest daughter's high school graduation.

Despite being so common, the threat of death still shocks. We have a tendency to look at people like Judith Wax and Olivier Chandon and sympathize because they had no time to prepare. It would be important, we think, to have all temporal and spiritual accounts squared, a balanced checkbook, a will in the hands of a competent lawyer, a thoroughly defrosted freezer, and no laundry in the hamper. Then we go about our business as if dying, for us, lurks around a faraway corner.

Awhile back I heard a minister tell about visiting a woman who had spent a lifetime amassing a fine collection of antique furniture. Thinking to please her, he complimented her on it.

"It's just furniture," she replied. Later he learned that she'd known she was dying. In what moment, do you suppose, did she cross the line from caring very much about furniture to not caring at all? When the doctor had said, "I'm sorry"?

Some might envy her advance warning, thinking she had time to ready herself, whereas others do not—but we *all* have advance warning. If the soul is an eternal flame, the body is a candle: It may burn brightly and steadily from top to bottom until the flame laps up the last bit of wax and expires, it may suffocate under the silver snuffer when the dinner party's over, or the flame may flicker once and vanish when an unexpected gust blows in through an open window. That it will go out should come as no surprise; the timing is what shocks—a room suddenly dark, a wick suddenly cold.

For all we know, we have only today to settle accounts, only today to ask forgiveness from a child whom we've wronged, only today to spend in the park instead of the office, only today to read bedtime stories, only today to write a letter to be opened by a son or daughter on the day he or she marries or has a child of his or her own.

For all we know, we have only today to decide what really matters—and what's "just furniture."

There Are Things Money Can't Buy

God was gentle and loving and exhibited great humor in that first year of my unemployment, as He guided me into a realization that my work here on earth was much, much more than what I did to earn a paycheck. Still, the world keeps trying to slap a monetary value on every job.

A recent estimate of how much a homemaker is worth put the value at $26,000 annually. That supposedly would cover the cost if you fell off a bridge and your family members were forced to hire others to do the chores that you do for free. You know: shopping, cooking, cleaning, mending—that sort of thing.

Well, $26,000 is pocket change compared to what it would *really* cost to replace Mom. If you were to take inventory of the average homemaker's day-in, day-out schedule, write up an accurate description of the job, and run want ads, nobody of sound mind would apply. Add to that the fact that about half of us work outside our homes either full or part time, and illegal aliens have better benefits.

If they were honest, the ads would read something like this:

✻ WANTED: chef-chauffeur-cheerleader. Must stock freezer with casseroles and snacks; prepare at least one nutritionally balanced hot meal a day, even though half the family won't be there to eat it; be on call to rush to doctor, dentist, or bank; attend soccer games in freezing rain; and dash to school with coat over bathrobe when child calls and says, "Mom, I forgot my homework." Pays $0 an hour. No sick days.

✲ WANTED: police officer-FBI agent-social worker-judge. Should be able to think of creative ways to discipline children who watch TV with the sound off when they're supposed to be in bed, and who leave wads of gum in their pants pockets. Should have the nose of a German shepherd for sniffing out falsehoods, and the wisdom of Solomon for dispensing appropriate measures of justice and mercy. Pays $0 per hour, double if incident involves major property damage to neighbor's house or yard.

✲ WANTED: accountant-secretary-marketing consultant to manage family budget, forge husband's name on birthday cards, and choose wedding and Christmas gifts for husband's family members, even though he does not know what size they wear or what colors they hate. Pays $0 per hour. Triple overtime if relatives compliment husband on his great taste, and he says, "Thank you."

✲ WANTED: maid with temperament of a St. Bernard and patience of St. Francis of Assisi. Must listen to husband complain about what a tough day he had at work, then watch him crumple in front of the television set while she finishes the ironing, vacuums the living room, scrapes strawberry jam off the kitchen floor, and turns the house upside down, because she has a laundry basket filled with 35 socks, and none of them match. Pays $0 an hour.

Got the idea? Nobody would volunteer to do what we do for free, and hardly anyone in the world could afford to hire us if we charged what we're worth. But money is not why we do it. We do it for love—and an occasional peanut-butter-and-jelly kiss. Most important, we do it because this is the work to which we've been appointed by the CEO: our Heavenly Father.

Bottom Line

List what you consider to be some of your most significant career accomplishments. Then list what you consider to be some of your most significant work (as in God-appointed) accomplishments. Ask Him to help you focus on areas of real and lasting importance.

Career Accomplishments   *"Work" Accomplishments*

1. _____   1. _____

2. _____   2. _____

3. _____   3. _____

12

Is There Life After Rush Hour?

I WAS SITTING IN A CAR DEALERSHIP WAITING ROOM ON A FRIDAY morning, sipping instant coffee from a paper cup. I could see though the window that it was snowing and the roads were icing up. When I'd given my car keys to the service department employee who wrote the work order, I said I had to be home by 11:30 A.M. in order to meet my daughter when she got off the kindergarten bus. "No problem!" he had said cheerily. So why was I nervous?

The television set in the waiting room was on, and Geraldo was interviewing—wouldn't you know it?—sexual deviants.

Terrific. I was planning to use the car repair time to catch up on my Bible reading. How was I supposed to concentrate on Moses tramping through the wilderness, with Geraldo tramping through the depths of human degradation? The worst of it was—Geraldo was fairly interesting.

Frustration churned within me, and the voice in my head that makes speeches said something like this: *OK, Lord. You know how I intended to spend this time. After caring for a sick child for several days and falling behind in all my regu-*

lar work, I really was looking forward to spending some quiet time with You. There's no phone here to interrupt me, and there are no household chores tempting me away. So what happens? It's sweeps month for the networks, and I'm a captive in this waiting room with total strangers, being bombarded with information that's almost too embarrassing to discuss with my husband! What's the deal?

A voice inside seemed to say, "Be still."

But God, You're not listening. I reserved this time for You! You know how much I've been looking forward to reading Your Word. Why aren't You paying attention?

Once again the voice seemed to say, "Be still."

OK, God. I'll give it a try, but I don't understand why I can't have some peace and quiet here. After all, I was trying to be obedient and study my Bible.

And the voice seemed to say, "Go ahead."

So I read, chapter after chapter after chapter. The noise was distracting, but one woman left when her car was ready, and after several uncomfortable minutes I finally mustered enough courage to ask my remaining companion, a man in his 40s, if I might turn down the volume.

He agreed and seemed relieved. I read steadily for an hour, and when I looked up it had stopped snowing. When my name was called, I felt as quiet and rested as if I'd had a nap.

I don't know about you, but I come up with lots of excuses as to why I'm not spending enough time studying God's Word and listening for His voice. That day in the car dealership, though, I realized that His quiet, gentle voice can drown out the noisiest interference, if only I allow it.

If I wait for the "perfect" quiet time to study and pray, weeks will pass. The world is tugging at my pant leg, just like a persistent toddler who can never get enough of my attention, and just like the editor who used to insist that I churn out 5 or 6 or 20 more paragraphs before heading for home. That world will never calm down long enough for me to be able to hear God's voice. That's why it's important that *I* learn to be still, inside.

Be Still, and Know That He Is God

Several times in my Bible I read the words "be still." When I'm tempted to seize control of a volatile situation, I can turn to Exod. 14:14, which says, "The LORD will fight for you; you need only to be still." In another instance, when the Israelites were close to being overcome with grief, the Levites calmed them by saying, "Be still, for this is a sacred day" (Neh. 8:11).

When employers treat me unfairly, I can rely on this promise: "Be still before the LORD and wait patiently for him; do not fret when men succeed in their ways, when they carry out their wicked schemes" (Ps. 37:7).

Do newspaper headlines regarding wars and rumors of wars frighten me? I can turn to Zech. 2:13 and read, "Be still before the LORD, all mankind, because he has roused himself from his holy dwelling."

How can I dwell on the fearful events of this earth, when I remember this account of our Lord's encounter with the forces of nature?—"He got up, rebuked the wind and said to the waves, 'Quiet! Be still!' Then the wind died down and it was completely calm" (Mark 4:39).

How I long to be completely calm! If only I could learn to obey Him as swiftly as do the wind and the waves!

For some reason, though, I keep slipping back into my worry mode, and that's when I need a reminder.

Good Friday Goes Bad

One of those reminders hit me full force on what might have been the worst Good Friday I ever spent.

Ruth, an elderly friend, lay in a hospital 30 miles away with a broken hip. Her family was scattered, and many of her friends were older and found it difficult to visit, so I decided to make the effort.

Since it was a holiday, I planned carefully. I would drop off some Easter flowers, swap news, give her a hug, and be on my way. That would leave plenty of time to eat a leisurely family dinner and make it to church in time for the Communion service.

Thanks to freeway construction, faulty directions, and a barricaded parking lot, it took nearly an hour and a half to reach the hospital, but I was still in pretty good shape as far as my schedule was concerned. At least I would have been, if Ruth had been in her room.

I waited, chatted with a couple of aides, and watered the flowers I had brought, plus the rest of the plants. Just as I was composing a note, a nurse wheeled Ruth in. We chatted for several minutes, and about the time I thought I should be going, she asked if I'd mind getting her favorite shoes.

"No problem," I said, thinking they must be under the bed, or in the closet on the other side of the room. "Where are they?"

They were 20 miles away, in her apartment, which is located in a high-rise in downtown Detroit.

She explained that the doctor wanted her to start walking, and she thought she could do a better job of it in her favorite sturdy shoes.

Calling home from a pay phone, I told my family to eat without me. Following the main avenue that rings the city, I passed the mansions and banks along the lake shore, then drove by boarded-up businesses and stores with barred windows and finally made my way to the downtown area. Ruth lived in a stately building where security is so tight that housekeepers have a sign-in sheet at the front desk, but I managed to talk my way past the guard.

I felt like a burglar rummaging through her closet, and it took quite awhile to locate the shoes. I made it out of the building just in time for afternoon rush hour—bumper-to-bumper, tire to tire, fist to fist.

This is just great, I thought. Why today? I should be reflecting on things of sublime eternal consequence, and here I am, wishing I could vaporize the city bus blocking my lane. And for what? There have to be a hundred better ways to spend Good Friday.

So I tried to think of one, but I couldn't. Locked into a jam of steaming cars and exasperated drivers, I thought about the walks my friend and I had taken in the garden behind her apartment building, watching the boats on the river, laughing at the ducks, admiring the roses—and suddenly, stuck on a crowded avenue in an overheating car with Ruth's shoes on the seat beside me seemed the best of all places to be.

I missed the Communion service that Good Friday, but I spent a long time communing with my Savior. As horns blared, and cars, trucks, and buses jockeyed for position, I felt waves of peace crashing over my troubled spirit. In the midst of confusion, at last I was still.

What might have been the worst Good Friday I ever spent turned out to be the best.

In the following months there were times I doubted Ruth would walk again, but she did. Last summer we walked all around the garden, a quarter of a mile, when the roses were in bloom. She leaned against my arm to steady herself, but her steps were firm, and she wore her favorite sturdy shoes.

God's Word says, "Be still, and know that I am God; I will be exalted among the nations, I will be exalted in the earth" (Ps. 46:10).

The world offers a number of prescriptions for those of us who suffer from the pressures and stresses of life, but all of them are temporary. The only permanent cure is this: Be still and know that He is God.

Slowing Down After Rush Hour

It has been seven years since I reset my alarm clock after deciding to quit rush hour entirely. I've had some time to reflect on the decision, and I've come to three conclusions:

1. The skills we women learn in school and in the workplace are not wasted when we stay home with children. Not only is raising a child an exciting and fulfilling career in itself, it requires all the skills and education we worked so hard to accumulate.

2. Being a mom is the best job on earth. If you're expecting a child right now for the first time, you may be wondering if the prophets of doom are right: that you'll be exhausted for the next 3, 4, maybe 21 years. The truth is—maybe so.

Most people who love their careers wind up tired at times, don't they? Caring for a child may well be the most physically and emotionally exhausting job a person can have, but it can also be the most rewarding. No doubt about it—you're in for the adventure of a lifetime.

3. Allowing yourself to be "adopted" by the Heavenly Father is the best career move any woman can make. If you, like my friend Thomas, have been changing the subject when confronted by the challenge to hear God's voice and follow Him, or if you've been putting off the decision until a more convenient time, I hope you'll reconsider.

There is no more important decision you can make, either for yourself or for your children, because your relationship with God, or lack of a relationship with Him, will affect your children in every area of their lives.

As Mothers, We're All Temps

A few months ago I toured Saarinen House, a 1930s home designed by Finnish architect Eliel Saarinen. It's located on the campus of Cranbrook Academy in Bloomfield Hills, Michigan.

After the guide led us into the dining room, he asked us to observe how all the elements within those four walls pulled together to lead our eyes upward to the focal point, an exquisite gold dome at the center of the room's ceiling.

That is exactly what I want my work as a mother to do. I want all the lessons and experiences and conversations and special times with my child to lead her eyes upward to the focal point of my life, my Heavenly Father.

Sometimes we get so caught up in the stress of deadlines, to-do lists, broken appliances, and uncooperative spouses and children, that we lose sight of what this parenting job assignment is all about. This is particularly true for women like me, who are constantly pulled from two directions: the commitment to home and family, and the desire to use our God-given abilities in the marketplace.

My current little boss—the one with the milk mustache—has already informed me that she'll be getting her driver's permit in the year 2000 (it's only fair to warn you now, so you can get off the road). What a painfully clear reminder that my current career is brief—and that I'd better make the most of it while I have the opportunity!

Bottom Line

Prayer: *Father, thank You for the opportunity to use my skills and experience in this fascinating and challenging career of motherhood. I look to You for guidance, as I guide the steps of this little one. I look to You for wisdom, as I try to share what I know. I look to You for confidence, as I learn what it means to love wholly, selflessly, and unconditionally. Most of all, thank You for being a terrific Parent. It's great being a mother, and I truly love being Your child. Amen.*

Notes

Chapter 6

1. Interview by author with Phyllis Gillis, author of *Entrepreneurial Mothers* (New York: Rawson Associates, 1984).

Chapter 10

1. Interview by author on WMUZ-FM (Detroit) with Kevin Leman author of *Keeping Your Family Together When the World Is Falling Apart* (New York: Delacorte Press, 1992).